Smart Solutions

for saving money & time

The Best Tips, Formulas & Solutions from the *Skinflint News* columns & newsletter

Melodie Moore

Copyright 1995 by Melodie Moore
Published by Skinflint Publishing, Inc.
Post Office Box 818
Palm Harbor, Florida 34682-0818

Printed in the U.S.A.

10 9 8 7 6

Library of Congress Catalog-in-Publication Data

Moore, Melodie.
  Smart Solutions/by Melodie Moore.
      p. cm.
  ISBN 0-8431-3471-2
  1. Consumer education. 2. Home economics I.
Moore, Melodie.
II. Title.
TX335.M653   1995   92-37308
640'.73-dc20   CIP

NOTICE: The information contained in this book is true and
complete to the best of our knowledge. All recommendations
are made without any guarantees on the part of the author or
of Skinflint Publishing, Inc. The author and publisher
disclaim all liability in connection with the use of this
information.

Table of Contents

1

Food,
Fabulous
Food

1

FOOD, FABULOUS, FOOD!

FRUIT

If bananas are starting to turn brown before you can eat them, put them in the refrigerator. The cold air will kill cells in the skin turning it brown, but the banana inside will stay fresh for several more days.

When making a recipe that calls for bananas (i.e., banana bread) if you do not have any over ripe bananas ask the produce manager for them. They may have some on hand in the stockroom waiting to be thrown away. If so, they will either give them to you FREE or sell them to you at a give-away price.

Buy grapes when they are on sale and freeze them. Frozen grapes are a fun and nutritious snack that both children and adults will enjoy. Add frozen grapes to any type of punch to keep the drink cold without diluting it.

To keep fresh fruit from discoloring, keep a spray bottle filled with half water and half lemon juice in the refrigerator. Whenever you cut up fresh fruit, spray it with the lemon water. This is quicker and easier than dipping fruit into lemon juice and you'll use less lemon juice with better results.

Don't throw away citrus rinds! Simmer them in water on your stove top for an inexpensive air freshener. The clean, fresh aroma will make your house smell wonderful.

Submerging a lemon, lime or other citrus fruit in hot water for 15 minutes before squeezing will yield almost twice the amount of juice. Or you can heat citrus in the microwave for about 15 to 20 seconds before squeezing.

When lemons or limes are bargain priced, buy extras and freeze the juice in ice cube trays. Then when citrus is out of season and the price is very high, you can use the juice cubes instead. You will be surprised at how "fresh" the frozen juice tastes.

Instead of throwing citrus rinds away, freeze a few of the rinds whole. Then when a recipe calls for a zest of lemon or orange you can use the frozen skin. Use a potato peeler to peel off small pieces of the rind. The frozen rind will be much easier to make into zest than a fresh rind.

When you buy a fresh pineapple let it sit on the countertop until it starts to smell like a ripe pineapple; then turn it upside down so the juice drains back into the entire fruit. You'll be amazed at how sweet and juicy the pineapple tastes.

Smart Reader Solution
I buy apples in a big bag when they are on sale. I feed them to my kids as a snack with peanut butter on top. It is an inexpensive

treat that they love. I also make apple sauce without even cooking the apples. Simply drop pieces of peeled apple in the blender and add a little lemon juice. You can add some honey or sugar if the apples are not sweet enough, or a touch of nutmeg or cinnamon make it taste yummy.

VEGETABLES
Don't throw away limp carrots or celery. To make them crisp again, soak the vegetables in ice water for 30 minutes.

Instead of buying a steamer for vegetables, you can steam vegetables the easy way. Simply place the veggies in a metal colander, then place the colander over a saucepan of boiling water. It works just like a steamer but doesn't cost any more money or take up extra cabinet space.

When making mashed potatoes, save the water and add it back to the potatoes as you mash them. It is cheaper than adding milk and your potatoes will be hot, creamy and delicious. Use the rest of the water as "free fertilizer". Let the water cool down to room temperature and use it to water house plants.

Get more for your money when making mashed potatoes. Don't peel the potatoes. Unpeeled potatoes make healthy, delicious mashed potatoes. Just wash and trim thoroughly, boil, and mash as usual.

Don't toss out leftover mashed potatoes. Freeze dollops of them and store in zipper-type freezer bags. You can use them later to make potato cakes or use them to thicken soups stews, gravies and sauces.

Vegetables will stay fresher in your refrigerator if you line your crisper section with newspapers or place a towel in the bottom. The newspapers or towel will absorb excess moisture and help the vegetables stay crisp. You can also wrap individual vegetables in newspapers to keep them crisp.

Save margarine wrappers (in the refrigerator or freezer) and use the margarine left on the paper to butter ears of corn. They also work great for rubbing the outside skins of potatoes before you bake them. You will be surprised at how much margarine (or butter) you have been tossing away!

To speed baking time and save energy, cut baking potatoes in half and place them cut side down on a baking sheet before placing them in the oven. They will cook much faster this way. For added flavor, place a pat of butter or margarine under each half.

Store fresh mushrooms in a brown paper bag in the refrigerator. If you buy mushrooms in a plastic bag or package, take them out of the wrapping and place them into a paper bag to make them last longer. The paper bag absorbs some of the moisture and prevents spoilage.

To make onions last longer don't store them near potatoes. Moisture from the potatoes will cause onions to sprout. The best way to store onions is hanging in old pantyhose. Drop the onions in the hose and tie a knot between each one. Then you can snip off onions one at a time as you need them.

Get together with friends and neighbors and buy fruit and vegetables from a wholesaler (see phone book for one in your area) by the case. It's much fresher and cheaper than what you can get at the grocery store.

LEFTOVERS
Tape a piece of paper on the refrigerator door to keep a list of leftovers inside. This way you will remember to eat what's inside before it turns into a science experiment!

To save money make "garbage soup." (Never call it garbage soup in front of family members!) Keep a container in the freezer and add leftover meat, gravy, rice and any vegetables. Add broth or tomato soup base (I make home-made tomato soup base) for a delicious soup that is a little different each time.

Save the cookie crumbs left at the bottom of the cookie jar and the cereal crumbs left in the bottom of the box. They make the best (and cheapest) topping for ice cream.

Eat leftover dinner rolls or biscuits for break-fast. Heat in the toaster or oven and add some butter and jam and you have a quick, inex-pensive breakfast.

FROZEN FOODS
Keep foods such as strawberries, pork chops, hamburgers and chopped vegetables from sticking together in the freezer by placing them in a single layer on a baking sheet and freezing until firm. Remove from the baking sheet when frozen solid and store in freezer containers to use as needed.

When you buy frozen vegetables you should be able to feel the individual vegetables inside the bag. Don't buy a bag if you can't; the package probably has thawed at some point before being re-frozen. The re-frozen veg-etables can have an off taste and they will not have as many nutrients.

To make ice cream last longer, place a piece of waxed paper, plastic wrap or aluminum foil on top of the ice cream once the container is opened. This will prevent ice crystals from forming on the ice cream and keep it fresh tasting longer.

Use the lids of plastic margarine, sour cream or cottage cheese containers to make perfectly shaped hamburger patties. Wrap the patty and lid with freezer wrap before freezing. You can wash the lids and use them over and over.

To make inexpensive popping corn pop bigger and stay fresh longer, store it in the freezer. You don't even have to thaw out the popcorn before popping it.

BREAD
Place a rib of celery in the bag with day old bread to make it fresh again. Leave the celery in the bag to keep the bread fresh longer.

Bread crumbs can be used in recipes to substitute for oatmeal. This is a great way to use up crusts.

Q. My bread quickly gets mold on it and I have to throw it away. Short of keeping it in the freezer, what can I do to keep it from getting moldy?

A. Keep bread in a bread box or cabinet that allows some air to circulate. Without air, the bread will quickly develop (and spread) mold. If you have a bread box that does not have any holes to circulate air, you may want to cut some small holes into the box yourself.

DRINKS
Make your own inexpensive flavored coffee by adding cocoa, cinnamon sticks, almonds, vanilla flavoring or anything else that suits your taste.

To make frozen juice more appealing, mix it in the blender. This mixing method makes it a light and frothy drink. Pour it into some special glasses and you have a very special (and inexpensive) treat. Children of all ages will love this treat.

Instead of buying expensive flavored sparkling water, you can make your own. Buy inexpensive store brand club soda and add juice or a few drops of fruit extract (my favorite flavors are strawberry and lemon) to make a non-fattening, inexpensive drink.

After opening a can of fruit (pears, pineapples, peaches, cherries, etc.) don't pour the juice down the drain. Instead, add the juice to whatever store bought juice you have in the refrigerator. The added juice will stretch your juice and add flavor.

Freeze leftover tea or any other drink your family likes in ice cube trays. Then use these cubes for a drink that does not get diluted as the ice melts.

To make your own flavored teas, make a pitcher of iced tea and add lemonade, punch, orange juice. It's much cheaper than the expensive flavored teas that are so popular.

When a recipe calls for wine you can substitute cranberry or grape juice. For white wine substitute apple juice. The juice saves money, tastes great and you probably already have some on hand!

If you prefer an expensive brand of coffee, try mixing your favorite brand half and half with a lower priced brand. The rich flavors of your favorite brand will still come through and you probably won't be able to taste the difference.

Save the leftover coffee from this morning and use it to add color to the gravy for dinner tonight! To make dark rich looking gravy, add a couple of tablespoons of brewed coffee (or a pinch of freeze dried coffee) to the gravy.

After coffee has perked, pour the hot coffee into a thermos bottle or a thermos coffee carafe (which has been warmed with hot water). The coffee will not get bitter and you will save electricity. Do this instead of adding salt to the coffee if you have hypertension.

Q. Is all bottled water spring water? I have been paying extra to buy bottled water and a friend told me that I was wasting my money because it is just tap water. I assumed that it was spring water but the label does not say exactly where the water is from.

A. If the label on bottled water does not specify that it comes from a natural spring, it usually is tap or well water that has been chemically treated and purified. You can buy purified drinking water from a machine for about 25 cents per gallon when you fill your own containers.

Soda Pop Tips

Q. I like to buy soda in 2 liter bottles but frequently the soda will end up flat before we drink the whole bottle. Do you have any tips for keeping the fizz in soda pop?

A. The best way I have found to keep the fizz in a two liter bottle is to put the cap on loosely, then squeeze the plastic bottle until the remaining liquid comes close to the top of the bottle. Then quickly close the cap tightly. With very little air in the bottle, it will take much longer for your soda to go flat. This trick will work until the bottle is about 3/4 empty.

When you do find that your soda is flat, don't throw it away. Instead freeze the flat soda in an ice cube tray and use them the next time you drink the same flavor soda. The cubes won't dilute your favorite soft drink.

MILK TIPS

You can extend the shelf life of milk by about 10 days past the expiration date. Before the expiration date (and if it's not spoiled), micro-wave milk (in the carton or microwave con-tainer) on high until the temperature reaches 160 degrees. (One cup of milk takes about 1 1/2 minutes.) Don't let the milk boil. Refrigerate immediately.

Instead of pouring out milk that is about to go out of date, pour the milk into an ice cube tray and freeze it. Then use the milk cubes for baking or to cool down hot coffee or hot cocoa.

To make milk last several days past the expiration date, add a pinch of salt. The salt will not affect the taste of the milk but it will keep it from spoiling as fast.

When milk starts to go sour, there's no need to throw it out. Don't drink it, but it's safe to use in cooking. Use it right away in cake batter, cookie dough or pancake batter. You can also use it in recipes calling for buttermilk.

Instead of buying expensive buttermilk for recipes, use regular milk and add one tablespoon of vinegar to each cup of milk. Let the mixture stand for one half hour before using.

When you think the chocolate syrup container is completely empty, fill the container with milk and shake. You'll get every last bit of syrup out of the container. You can drink the chocolate milk cold or heat it for hot chocolate.

MISC.
Whenever possible, cook in cast iron pots and skillets. They add extra iron to your food

without any extra cost!

Use round dishes when cooking in the microwave. You'll use less energy because the food cooks more effectively and evenly.

To make salad dressing last longer put about a tablespoon of dressing in the bottom of each salad bowl. Then add the salad, and just before eating, lightly toss the salad to coat the greens. You may be surprised at how far a little dressing can go. This saves money and calories!

You pay a very high price for some quick, convenience foods. Take for example rice packaged ready for the microwave; it can be as much as 1500 times more expensive than rice bought in bulk!

To revive stale marshmallows, place them in an airtight container with a slice of fresh bread. Give it a couple of days and they will be as good as new. If a recipe calls for small marshmallows and you only have large ones you can easily use kitchen scissors to cut them to size. Dip the scissors in hot water if they become sticky.

Buy a pot of growing parsley. Snip just what you need; there is no waste, it's always fresh and it even looks pretty in the kitchen!

If you make gravy and it turns out lumpy

don't throw it away; use your electric mixer to smooth out the lumps.

When you buy marshmallows, store them in the freezer. Marshmallows won't dry out when they are frozen. Just pour out the amount you need and keep the bag in the freezer. Marshmallows will thaw out quickly; by the time you have mixed the other ingredients, the marshmallows will be ready to add to your recipe.

EGGS
Always buy eggs from a refrigerated egg case. Eggs bought at room temperature will spoil much faster. Every day an egg is stored at room temperature it loses more quality than it will during a week of refrigeration.

To save an egg that cracks as you boil it, pour some salt directly on the crack and return it to the boiling water. The salt will help seal the crack and keep most of the egg white inside.

You don't need an expensive egg poaching machine to make perfectly round pouched eggs; use an empty tuna can! Remove the top and bottom with a can opener. Drop the can in a pan of boiling water and crack an egg or two into it and you will have beautiful poached eggs made the Skinflint way. Add a drop or two of vinegar to the boiling water to keep the egg whites from spreading.

To keep eggs fresh longer, the best way to

store them is in the refrigerator in the original container they were purchased in. These containers help them stay colder in the refrigerator. One of the worst places to store eggs is in the refrigerator door. Every time the door is opened, the eggs will get a blast of warm air.

Q. Why do brown eggs cost more than regular white eggs. Are they better quality eggs?

A. There is no difference in taste or quality of brown eggs verses white eggs. The only difference is most brown eggs are laid by hens descended from Rhode Island Reds. They are larger birds, so they eat more food. That's why brown eggs generally cost more than white ones.

CHEESE
Instead of throwing away hard cheese, grate it and use on your favorite vegetables and casseroles. Mix the cheese with stale bread crumbs for a delicious topping.

Cottage cheese will stay fresher longer if you store the carton upside down in the refrigerator. Just make sure the lid is on tight!

To prevent cheese from drying out and molding, wrap it in a moist paper towel with a small amount of cider vinegar. Store the cheese in a sealed plastic bag or airtight container. You may need to add water or a drop or two of cider after a use or two.

BAKING

When baking cookies, make a double batch and freeze part of the batter in a freezer container or a plastic margarine bowl with a tight fitting lid. The batter will keep for approximately 6 to 8 weeks. When you are ready for some hot, homemade cookies thaw out the dough and bake a small batch.

Sprinkle frosted cookies with gelatin to add color instead of buying expensive colored sprinkles.

To keep your flour bug-free, store it in the freezer! Coffee stays fresher there, too.

Q. Please tell me how to make cake flour from regular flour. Can I use regular flour instead of cake flour?

A. You can't really make cake flour from all-purpose flour. All purpose flour is a blend of hard and soft wheat. Cake flour is a finely milled soft wheat flour. You can use all-purpose flour in the place of cake flour when baking. Use seven-eighths of a cup for every cup of cake flour called for in the recipe. Sift the flour at least twice to make it lighter.

When baking a chocolate cake, add a little flour to the container that you melted chocolate in. The flour will get the last bit of chocolate out of the pan and into the cake batter. I hate to waste anything, especially chocolate!

Olive oil kept on the shelf can become rancid quickly due to exposure to light. Tightly wrap the oil bottle, including the neck up to the bottom of the cap, with heavy foil. The oil will keep for many months without refrigeration.

To "save" a dry cake, poke holes in the top with a toothpick and pour a small amount of fruit juice in the holes.

Use margarine wrappers to grease baking pans so that the margarine left on the wrapper will not be wasted. Place margarine wrappers in a plastic bag in the freezer until you need to grease a pan.

Don't throw away brown sugar that is as hard as a rock; instead place a piece of fresh bread into the box or bag and close tightly. The moisture from the bread will soften the brown sugar so it can be used.

Save cereal box liners to use as waxed paper. They're especially good for rolling out pie crusts.

When you buy cooking oil, you can save money if you will pour the oil into a squirt bottle. You will find that you can easily control the amount used and will use less. Which not only saves money but it also saves calories. Save an old squirt bottle (such as a honey bear or a squeeze mustard bottle) and use it to squirt the oil.

Don't throw away cookies that are burnt on the bottom. Instead, scrape off the burned part and they taste just fine. You can use a cheese grater to remove the burned portion. If the cookies crumble, save them to use as ice cream topping.

MICROWAVE TIPS

Q. When I heat leftover bread or rolls in the microwave they tend to get tough and dry. When I heat muffins or pastries they get soggy on the bottom. I always try to eat leftovers, but I wish I knew how to make them taste better.

A. Heating too long makes breads or rolls tough and dry. Heat bread or rolls for about 15 seconds. Then heat for an additional few seconds if they are not hot. To prevent your muffins or pastries from getting soggy on the bottom, heat them on a paper towel, or if you prefer, you can heat them on a paper (not foam) plate.

Q. Can I pop regular popcorn in the microwave? The little microwave bags are so expensive.

A. Regular popcorn can be cooked in the microwave if you use microwave-safe containers made especially for popping corn. Don't try to pop it in a brown paper bag. Kernels can scorch and cause a fire inside the microwave oven if brown bags or other improper containers are used. Shop around and you should be able to find an inexpensive microwave popping container. It will quickly pay for itself if you enjoy popcorn.

BREAKFAST
For a nice change from the usual routine, serve breakfast for dinner. Pancakes, French toast and eggs are quick, easy and inexpensive.

If you run out of syrup, instead of making an extra trip to the store, make your own topping out of jelly. Add a pat of butter and a little water to fruit jelly. Heat in the microwave or on the stove top. This tastes delicious on pancakes and French toast. It is also a much cheaper substitute for flavored syrups.

Make your own flavored pancake and waffle syrup: Stir one cup of corn syrup and four tablespoons of your favorite jam or preserves in a saucepan over low heat. Store any leftover syrup in the refrigerator.

Make your own instant oatmeal and save. Microwave old-fashioned or quick oatmeal right in the bowl. Add a squirt of honey or some vanilla extract and cinnamon for added flavor. It doesn't take any longer to make than the expensive, prepackaged 'instant' variety.

You'll find this is a painless way to save money.

Low Cost Cereal Recipe

Q. The cost of cereal has gone sky high. What can I do to reduce my costs?

A. The price of cereal has increased dramatically. It is estimated that since 1983 prices have increased 90 percent! Much of the extra costs are for advertising. Look for store brands to save money. There are also national brands such as Malt O Meal and even Quaker Oats that offer a low priced cereal in a bag instead of a box. One of the best ways to save is to make your own granola type cereal. Try this recipe. I'll bet even your kids will love it; and the best news is it costs about half the price of packaged cereals.

Heat oven to 375 degrees. Place 2 tablespoons margarine in a square (8 or 9 inch) baking pan; heat until melted. In a bowl mix together 1 1/2 cups old fashioned oats, 1/4 cup sliced almonds (optional), 3 tablespoons brown sugar and 1 tablespoon sunflower seeds. Toss with margarine in pan. Bake for 15 to 20 minutes or until golden brown. Stir once during cooking. Add 1/2 cup raisins. When cooled, store in an airtight container for up to one month. You can eat it as a snack or pour milk over it for a delicious low cost breakfast cereal.

MEAT

Marinate meats in a plastic bag instead of a pan. By placing the meat in a bag, you will be able to use about half of the usual amount of marinate. Turn the bag over several times during the marinating process.

When freezing ground meat, pack it into meal-size portions and shape the meat as flat as the zip-type freezer bag will allow. The meat will freeze and thaw much faster when you do it this way.

When making salmon patties substitute mackerel instead. The mackerel is less expensive and it tastes just as good.

Meat fibers are broken down and tenderized by vinegar. Less expensive cuts of meat can be used in most recipes without sacrificing flavor. Soak the meat in vinegar overnight; If desired, rinse off the vinegar before cooking.

NUTS/SNACKS

Q. Is there a way to make stale peanuts taste fresh again? I tried heating the in the microwave and it did not help.

A. Place the stale peanuts (or other nuts) in an uncovered shallow pan and bake in the oven at 250 degrees for 5 to 10 minutes. The heat from the oven will freshen them right up.

Crackers will stay crisp longer when stored in

the refrigerator. Be sure they are tightly wrapped.

Pudding Tips
Instead of buying expensive frozen pudding pops, make your own. I have found that the pudding pops taste best if you dilute the pudding with one cup of milk before freezing. The milk gives them a creamy texture and stretches your pudding.

Don't buy pudding in expensive individual containers. Make your own pudding and pour it into small plastic containers. I use the small margarine bowls. It is still a fun treat for the kids because they always love snacks in individual containers.

Q. I make pudding for an inexpensive dessert or snack. How can I prevent skin from forming on top? I have tried covering it while it cools but the skin still forms.

A. To prevent skin from forming on your pudding, spread a thin layer of cream or melted butter on top right after cooking. Stir and the skin will disappear.

THE SWEET STUFF
If whipped cream will not whip, don't throw it out; instead add the white of an egg or a little cornstarch to the whipping cream to make it whip.

If you use powdered sugar instead of granu-lated sugar when making whipped cream, the whipped cream will last longer since it will not separate as quickly.

Don't be tempted to buy sugar packets for convenience. One packet of sugar can cost about 500 times as much as the same amount of sugar bought in a five pound bag.

Q. I've heard that you can make powdered sugar out of granulated sugar. Can you tell me how to do this? I never seem to have pow-dered sugar when I need it, but I always keep granulated sugar on hand.

A. It is very easy and fairly quick to make powdered sugar out of regular sugar. Simply take one cup of white granulated sugar and add 2 tablespoons of cornstarch; place in a blender on high for 2 minutes. Do not double this recipe. If you need more powdered sugar, make two batches.

If honey has crystallized, don't throw it away. Set the bottle in a pan of hot water. Heat on the stove over low heat until crystals disap-pear. You can use the same process for jelly and syrups. Watch the water closely and don't let it get too hot. Very hot or boiling water could crack glass jars or melt plastic ones.

THE SPICE OF LIFE (Herbs)
Growing your own herbs is not only a way to

save money but fresh herbs also add so much flavor to your recipes. You can start herbs from seeds or buy them in small pots. Look for inexpensive herbs at the grocery store or flea market. They look pretty and are an endless supply of inexpensive flavorings. Here are a few helpful hints on using herbs.

To mince herbs quickly, use sharp kitchen scissors, or chop with a very sharp knife.

The finer you mince fresh herbs, the more flavor you will get.

One tablespoon of fresh herbs equals one teaspoon of dried herbs.

For the most (and freshest) flavor, add herbs to soups or stews during the last 45 minutes of cooking time. Or save half of the herbs to stir in 10 minutes before the dish is done.

When using herbs in a thick cold mixture such as a dip or cheese spread, refrigerate it for several hours (or overnight) for the best flavor.

If you cut off more fresh herbs than you need, you can freeze the extra herbs in ice cube trays. Pour water over the fresh herbs and freeze in cubes. Then when you need the seasoning, drop in a cube or two. The frozen herbs will taste, almost like fresh picked.

Q. I've heard that you can make your own vanilla extract. I would like to try it. Can you tell me how to do it? Is it economical to make?

A. Yes you can make vanilla extract and it is a fairly simple task. Place one vanilla bean and a cup of brandy or vodka in an airtight, opaque container. Seal the container tightly and store in a dark place (such as the cupboard) for at least four weeks. To get the most flavor, break the bean into pieces and make sure each piece is covered with the brandy or vodka. The longer you leave the bean soaking, the stronger the vanilla flavoring will have. Remove the bean from the liquid. This home-made mixture can be substituted for vanilla extract in any recipe. If you can find vanilla beans for sale in bulk this can be economical. If bulk vanilla beans are not available in your local area an imitation vanilla extract probably will be the most economical choice.

To make spices stay fresh and full of flavor longer, store them in a cupboard or spice rack away from the heat of the stove or oven. Also avoid storing them in a window, since the heat of the sun will make them lose their flavor.

It is especially helpful to buy bulk spices when you just need a small amount for a recipe. It's crazy to buy a large jar that will last many years when you may never need it again.

Tips for Cheap Eating

Avoid habit buying. Always look for new or different alternatives that may be cheaper and better. Most people will buy practically the same items each week. Even products that were once the least expensive may be high priced when compared to other brands and sizes.

Never buy anything pre-sweetened. If you are going to buy sugar anyway, why pay four or five times more for the sugar? You can also better control the amount of sugar added. Some examples of pre-sweetened items are instant tea, cereal and packaged soft drinks.

Don't pay extra for fancy packaging. You may actually be paying more for the package than the contents! Look for packages that are re-cycled or can be recycled.

Don't be afraid to try store brands or generics. Start with the cheapest product (per ounce) and if the quality is not up to your standards, try the next cheapest. The store brands and even generic brands are often the same prod-ucts, supplied by the some companies, at much lower prices.

When cooking, always measure ingredients. You will get consistent results with your reci-pes and save money. Most people will add about twice as much as needed when they do not measure.

2

Tips for the Garden

GARDEN

Free Fertilizers
Ashes from your fireplace make an excellent fertilizer for bushes and trees.

After cooking vegetables in water, cool the water to room temperature and use it to water your house plants. Your plants will slurp up the vitamins!

Smart Reader Solution
It is cheaper to buy lawn fertilizer with moss or weed control than to buy the products separately. You can save money killing moss on walks and driveways by spraying the moss with bleach.

Plants
Don't waste money on special "grow lights" for indoor plants. Ordinary white fluorescent lights are cheaper, last longer and work just as well.

Save the top of a pineapple for a "free" house plant. Remove the fruit and a few of the bottom leaves. Place the stem in an inch or two of water for a couple of weeks. Once you have roots, you can plant it in a pot or outside (if you live in a warm climate).

Save water and save plants by knowing when to water them. Stick a pencil down in the dirt (be careful to avoid roots) in the flower or plant pot. If it comes out with dirt clinging to it; don't water. If it comes out dry and smooth; it needs a drink.

Save milk jugs to use as plant trays. Cut the jugs to the desired height and start your spring plants early. Make several holes in the bottom for drainage.

Use plastic shower caps that hotels give away to catch water drips from hanging plants. Place the shower cap over the bottom of the plant pot and then you don't have to worry about it dripping on the floor.

Save the plastic "peanuts" you get in packages and use them when you pot plants. A layer of them in the bottom of the pot is perfect for drainage.

Small flowering house plants such as African violets, begonias and bulbs (hyacinths, narcissus, tulips) make lovely centerpieces and not only cost less, but also last longer than fresh cut flowers.

Garden
Make several different plantings of the same vegetable, spaced several days apart. This will assure you fresh vegetables over a longer period of time.

Use plastic gallon milk or water jugs to drip irrigate your thirsty crops like tomatoes or cucumbers. Simply poke a few holes in the bottom and sink the jug up to its neck in the middle of the bed. Fill the jugs with water and it will seep through the ground to thirsty roots and not a drop of the water will be lost to evaporation.

To save money, plant strawberries. They are a perennial so they come back every year and produce additional plants.

The best food for your garden is compost. Grind leftover vegetables, eggshells and veg-etable peelings in the blender, then spread them around the garden.

When planting flowers this spring, place a layer of newspapers under the flowers. The paper will help keep weeds from popping up and they will also help hold moisture in the soil.

To make fresh flowers last longer, place them in the refrigerator when you are not at home. When you remove them from the refrigerator don't place them in a drafty area or in direct sunlight.

Save out-of-shape or extra wire hangers to use as garden stakes. Use a wire cutter to make short stakes.

Use old pantyhose to tie up tomato plants. The hose won't cut into the vines and the price is right!

Make an inexpensive drip irrigation system for your garden out of an old leaky garden hose. Take an ice pick or nail and poke holes in the hose. Then lay the hose between the rows in your garden. Turn the water on low so that it slowly drips out through the holes into the ground.

Clean it Up!
For quick cleanups after gardening, working on the car, or playing outside, put the little leftover soap slivers in a mesh bag from the produce department and tie it to a water spigot outside. It saves on smudged doors and greasy doorknobs.

Don't throw away old rubber gloves with small holes in them. Use the old gloves to work in the garden, re-pot house plants or other "dirty" jobs. They will keep your fingernails clean and it does not matter that they are not water tight.

Before tackling a really greasy or messy job, scratch your fingernails in a bar of soap. Soap will help keep the dirt off your nails and you will be able to quickly clean up your hands after the job is done.

Weeds/Pests
To kill the weeds that grow in the sidewalk cracks, pour full strength vinegar on them.

The vinegar will kill the weeds and keep them from coming back for quite some time.

If you have problems with deer, rabbits and other animals eating vegetables out of your garden, ask your barber or beautician to save some hair clippings for you. Spread them around your garden and the animals will stay away from your vegetables or flowers.

Tools
Paint your garden tool handles a bright color (such as yellow, pink or orange). You will easily be able to spot the bright colors in the yard (no more lost tools) and when you loan tools to a friend or neighbor the different color will help them remember where to return the tool.

Make your own fertilizer spreader out of a large coffee can. Punch lots of holes in the bottom of the can. Use the plastic lid to hold the fertilizer inside the can; then remove the lid and shake to distribute the fertilizer.

Don't throw away an old pillow; instead cover it with a plastic bag and use it to cushion your knees when working in the yard or garden. When you are finished working, throw the plastic bag away and save the pillow for the next time you have yard work to do.

Seeds
If you would like a free packet of seeds, you

can participate in "Plant A Row for the Hungry", the nationally sponsored project to stop hunger in America. To get your free packet of seeds, send your request to Thompson & Morgan P. O. Box 1308, Jackson, NJ 08527. All they ask is that you donate some of the produce to a local soup kitchen, food bank, homeless shelter or day care center.

Q. How can I save extra seeds for next year? The seed packets always have too many seeds. I hate to plant too many or throw the seeds away because I know that I could use them next year. I saved some seeds in the original packets last year and they got wet and sprouted before I could plant them.

A. The best way to keep vegetable or flower seeds dry and organized is to store them in little bottles (baby food bottles are perfect) or plastic margarine containers that have a tight lid. Simply place the extra seeds into the clean, dry bottle or container and add a few tablespoons of flour or corn meal to the container. The flour or corn meal helps keep the seeds dry. Put the containers in a cool, dark place until you are ready to plant again. I tape a picture from the seed packet on the outside of the container so I know what seeds are inside the container. If the jar is clear just place the seed package inside folded so you can see what's inside.

3

Traveling
Skinflint
Style

THRIFTY TRAVEL TIPS

Lodging
When traveling, never accept the first price quoted for hotel or motel rooms or for car rentals. Tell them you are looking for the lowest price and ask what type of discounts they offer. Most offer membership discounts such as American Automobile Association (AAA) or American Association of Retired Persons (AARP) but some offer even better discounts for "family packages."

Use a pay phone to make calls rather than pay the hotel fee to have your phone turned on. Some hotels have extremely high phone rates for long distance charges. You never know what the rate is going to be. Use a calling card with your regular long distance company to save the most.

If you will be staying for a full week at your destination, try to find a condo or vacation cottage to rent instead of a hotel room. The rate will probably be cheaper and you'll have much more space and the extra added benefit of a full kitchen.

Always review your lodging, car rental or any other bill closely. Frequently you can find errors. Ask about any charges you are not certain about.

Visit relatives for free overnight lodging and

fun. Don't impose on them for many days; but a night or two will be fun for both without wearing out your welcome.

Stop at the state welcome center and pick up a discount hotel booklet. Many states offer a discount booklet for rooms that would other-wise go empty. The rates in these booklets are hard to beat.

Q. I recently went on a group tour with several other couples, one evening some of my friends in the group were discussing what neat souvenirs the shampoo, soaps and note pads in the hotel bathroom were. I was shocked that one of the ladies said she had a towel collection from hotels. To me, taking the towels is stealing. I like to get my fair share of freebies but I don't want to "cross the line." Where do you draw the line on what is fair game to take home and what is stealing?

A. Hotels and motels generally expect guests to take the shampoo, shower cap, soap and other "disposable" items on the bathroom tray; some even have signs to let you know. Once the bottles of shampoo or boxes of soap are open, the hotel must throw them away for safety reasons; so you might as well take what is left home with you to use. But taking the towels, ashtrays, ice buckets or other items that are not disposable, is "crossing the line" and the cost of replacing the missing items will end up costing everyone more in increased room rates.

Take To The Skies
To get the lowest airfare possible, call the airlines on a weekday. On weekends they often hike up fares to see if the competition will follow suit. If the other carriers don't match the increased prices, they usually will reduce the fares back down on Monday.

Q. What happens if an airline ticket is lost or destroyed? Can you get a replacement ticket or do you lose your money?

A. You should report a lost ticket immediately. For a fee of about $50, most carriers will issue a replacement ticket if you can prove that you bought the ticket. Some of the low fare air-lines do not issue tickets. They simply give you a confirmation number instead. This reduces paperwork and saves the airline big money.

Look for airline ticket bargains during the summer or just after major holidays. Most airlines will resort to discounting fares drasti-cally since ticket sales are slow.

Food
When traveling, stop at a large supermarket or grocery store for dinner. You can usually get a full meal at the delicatessen, including vegetables and dessert. Not only is it more nutritious, but it will probably be cheaper

than a burger and fries.

Eat a big breakfast when traveling and go lighter on lunch or dinner. Breakfast is typically the least expensive meal of the day.

Pack a cooler and shop for groceries and supplies along the way. Find a nice picnic area and enjoy a family picnic instead of spending big money each night on a restaurant meal.

Smart Reader Solution
For a quick travel lunch, make a sandwich, carrot sticks, fruit and a cookie or other snack. Arrange the lunch on a clean Styrofoam tray. Cover the tray with plastic wrap. Make one for each person traveling. You can stop almost anywhere and enjoy the quick lunch. The tray makes it easy to eat anywhere; even if you can't find a roadside table.

For fast food stops while traveling patronize restaurants that offer free refills. Then buy only the smallest size to save money.

Order ice water to drink with restaurant meals. It should be free and it will really make a difference in the total tab. Buy a pack of soft drinks at the grocery store and keep them in your cooler.

Take your own coffee pot and supplies to make fresh coffee in the motel each morning.

You can even take it a step further and take items such as a toaster and an electric skillet. Some families really economize on meals and spend the bulk of the vacation budget on special attractions or a longer (further) vacation destination.

Getting Around
Car Rental Tip: Reserve the lowest rate you can find on a compact car. You can almost always upgrade the car when you arrive and often the upgrade will be free. Most car rental companies have many more mid-sized and large cars than small ones. If a compact car is not available when you check in, ask to be upgraded to a larger car for free.

Call your insurance agent before renting a car to find out if you are insured while driving a rental. The insurance that rental agencies try to sell you is very expensive and in most cases in not necessary.

Don't opt for the rental car company to refill the gas tank. It may sound like a bargain but in reality they will charge you for a full tank of gas even if you turn in the car with some gas in it. Fill it up yourself before returning it to make sure you don't overpay.

Save time and possibly gas by writing down the major cities you will travel through. Post the notes on the dash so you can quickly look at it to make sure you are headed the right direction. Or highlight your map to make it easy to follow.

Check your car before heading out on a trip. If needed, tune it up and change the oil. Make sure your spare tire is filled with air. This will help avoid an expensive out of town breakdown. Check fluids, air pressure in all tires, belts and any other problem areas.

Miscellany
Use a travel agent to help you plan your trip. A good travel agent can save you money by searching for bargain destinations and looking out for the best deals.

Check with AARP (American Association of Retired Persons) or AAA (American Automobile Association) for travel advice, discounts, maps and other services. Both have lots of ways to help you save.

Travel to a destination that has lots of free activities. You can have fun, learn something interesting and save money.

Buy books to read on vacation at used book stores or garage sales. A new book bought at the airport will cost at least $5 for a paperback. Be prepared with your own magazines to read during any layovers or delays.

If you can leave for vacation without much notice, consider tour consolidators. They have some unbelievable deals but the tour may leave in less than 24 hours!

Always buy more film than you think you'll need when it is on sale at home. You can spend double or even triple the amount if you wait and buy film while on vacation.

Take some postcard stamps with you when you go on vacation. This way you won't waste time and money trying to find a post office or buying more stamps than you need.

Use rest-areas for breaks. They have free water and clean rest rooms, and no restaurants or gift shops to tempt you or your kids to spend money.

Do-it-yourself Home Repairs

HOME REPAIRS

PAINTING TIPS

To make it easier to open the paint can lid next time you need the paint, punch a few holes into the *inside rim*; this will allow the paint caught in the rim to drain back down into the can.

While painting, stretch a large rubber band around your paint can from the top of the can to the bottom. Use the rubber band to wipe the brush across to remove excess paint from the brush. The rubber band will keep paint from dripping all over, and it will keep the side and rim of the paint can clean.

Glue a paper plate on the bottom of the paint can to catch any drips.

After finishing a painting project, draw a line with your brush on the outside of the can at paint level. This will show both the color and the amount of paint left in the can.

To clean and soften hardened paintbrushes, simmer them in boiling vinegar for a few minutes before washing in warm, soapy water.

To clean paint from your hands, rub them with vegetable oil before washing with hot, soapy water. The oil works as good as a commercial paint remover or gasoline and it is much kinder to the skin.

When painting, put an old pair of socks over your shoes to protect them from paint splatters.

Wallpaper borders can cost up to $20 for five yards, so putting up a wallpaper border, even a small room, could easily cost several hundred dollars. Using a stencil and paint, you can get the same results for less money.

When painting ceilings, use plastic dry cleaning bags to keep lighting fixtures from getting splattered with paint.

When washing out paint brushes, pour a tablespoon of liquid fabric softener in the water and let them soak for a few minutes before the final rinse. This will make them soft and pliable for the next use.

REPAIRS
Save a bundle on costly repairs; Before calling a repairman when electrical equipment or an appliance breaks, call the customer service department of the company that makes the item. Many companies have trained representatives to answer questions and guide you through simple repairs over the telephone. Call the 800 Directory (1-800-555-1212) for toll free numbers.

When you need to make a small home repair, check out books or video tapes at the library to help you do the project yourself. Ask if your local "do-it-yourself" hardware store offers any free classes on the type of repair you are planning to do.

To quiet down a squeaky door hinge, apply several drops of vegetable oil. Blot excess oil with a paper towel or newspaper to keep it from dripping on the floor or carpet.

Always rub a little petroleum jelly or oil on screws or bolts before putting together an unassembled item. This way if you ever have to take the item apart it will be much easier.

To fix a loose knob on a dresser or chest of drawers, dip the screw portion of the knob into clear nail polish or shellac. When the nail polish or shellac dries, the knob will be set tightly.

Save old mascara tubes for quick touch-ups of black or brown painted surfaces. The old mascara works especially good for wood paneling.

5

Here's to your Health

HEALTH

The Drug Store

Remove the cotton as soon as a medicine bottle is opened to prevent germs from spreading from your hands to the cotton. The cotton in a bottle of aspirins or vitamins can spread a cold or flu to everyone in the family!

Ask your doctor to give you samples of any new drug prescribed. If he has samples available, you can make sure that the drug works for you and does not cause any undesirable side effects before buying a large supply that will be wasted. If he does not have samples of your particular drug, ask for a one week prescription first.

Smart Reader Solution

Don't buy those expensive "daily pill reminders" to keep track of daily doses of pills. Use empty film canisters instead. Once a week fill seven empty canisters with each day's dosage for the coming week and mark it with the appropriate day.

When treating yourself with an over-the-counter medication, always ask your pharmacist for advice. A pharmacist can advise you on the value and benefits of one product over another. He or she can also help you save money by recommending the right product and possibly a generic equivalent. A pharmacist can also explain the proper way to take the medication and make sure that the over-the-counter medication will not interfere with any prescription medications you take.

Don't pay extra for brand-name vitamins; you're just paying for advertising and more expensive packaging. The same few companies that actually make vitamins supply all the other companies that sell them under different brand names.

Smart Reader Solution
I asked the pharmacist of our local discount store to recommend a multi-vitamin for our family. He showed me a well-known vitamin and compared it to the store brand. Both had the exact same ingredients. The price, however, was one-half for the house brand. Second, a sample size container was available. The price per vitamin was cheaper in the sample sized bottles. Third, I use the cotton inside the bottle as a cotton ball for cosmetic uses.

Get more from your calcium supplement. You can double the amount of calcium your body absorbs when taking a calcium supplement by drinking a glass of orange juice when you take the supplement. The juice increases stomach acid, which helps to break down the calcium into a form that the body can easily absorb.

Several commonly prescribed medications

now have a generic version on the market that can save you up to 50 percent. Some of the more commonly prescribed drugs that now have generic versions are Tagamet, Halcion, Corgard, Anaprox, Naprosyn and more are scheduled soon. Ask your doctor if the medication you have been taking has a generic equivalent and if he recommends it.

Smart Reader Solution
I am 69 years old and I asked my doctor about what type of lotion to use for my extremely dry skin around my ankles, elbows and toes. He told me to forget about name brand lotions and simply massage olive oil into the dry areas. It works great!

Exercise
Check with local schools, hospitals, churches or women's clubs for free or inexpensive exercise classes. Meet some news friends, get in shape and save money at the same time!

Make your own inexpensive exercise video by setting the VCR to record aerobic or exercise shows on television. Find a show you like and tape several episodes. Then you can do a workout whenever you find the time.

Q. I exercise quite a bit and seem to get more than my share of athlete's foot. I spend a small fortune on over-the-counter medications. What can I do to save money and reduce my chances of getting athlete's foot?

A. To avoid athlete's foot, wear cotton socks, and if your feet perspire a great deal, add cornstarch to your socks and shoes (sprinkle on just like power) before working out. If you shower at a gym, always wear shoes (beach shoes or thongs) to significantly reduce your chances of getting athlete's foot.

First Aid
Freeze un-popped popcorn in small plastic bags to use for ice packs. It really works; no watery mess. When the popcorn is no longer cold, you can simply re-freeze it and use it again.

Keep a wet sponge in the freezer and you will have an emergency ice pack that is ready to go.

You can quickly grab a package of frozen vegetables (such as peas) to ice down a bump or bruise.

If you need a hot water bottle quickly but can't find one, try this homemade solution. Pour hot (not boiling) water into an empty plastic soda bottle and wrap it in a towel. You'll find quick relief without having to spend money on a hot water bottle.

Lower Health Care Costs
If you live near a medical or dental school, you may be able to take advantage of health and

dental services offered by the school as part of the students' training. The cost for these services will be very low; sometimes even free. The students are supervised and you will get the advantages of the newest procedures and practices.

When you must stay in the hospital overnight, you can save money by bringing your own toiletries and other items. The hospital will be more than happy to provide you with razors, toothpaste, tissues or other supplies, but the price will be staggering!

Check with your local health department for all sorts of free or low cost services. They may offer anything from cholesterol screening to free or reduced cost vaccinations and immunizations. Take advantage of these services as needed to save money.

Always wear sun block! The money you spend on sun block can save you big money in lower health care costs later in life. A tanned body make look good now; but the physical and financial costs of skin cancer are not worth it!

Even if your insurance pays your hospital and doctor bills, check them carefully for errors. If you have any discrepancies or questions be sure to find out the answers. This is one way we all can help to control the skyrocketing costs of health care.

Favorite Home Remedies
When you have a sinus headache or a stuffy nose, try this inexpensive home remedy. Dip a washcloth in hot water, wring out only enough to keep it from dripping, and place it over the upper half of the face. Press around the nose and eye sockets. When the cloth cools down, repeat. Continue doing this for 10 to 15 minutes. This will usually relieve the pressure that caused the headache. This is best done while lying down.

For indigestion, mix about one ounce of lemon juice in a glass of cold water and drink it. This is a quick and easy way to relieve the indigestion.

Smart Reader Solution
I keep a small bottle of very strong cold tea in the refrigerator for use on any sort of minor burn. The acid in tea is really beneficial in treating burns. This has been proven medically, which just shows that our Grandmothers really knew what they were talking about! I just love home remedies because they use common household items that you don't have to run out to a pharmacy and shell out a lot of money.

6

Beauty on a Budget

BEAUTY ON A BUDGET

Bath Time
Instead of buying expensive bath oil, make your own. Buy a generic bottle of baby oil and add a few drops of your favorite perfume. You can even add a drop of food coloring to make it look pretty.

To soften hard water and make an inexpensive relaxing bath, add one-half cup baking soda to your bath water. It makes a refreshing bath additive for just a few pennies.

To make your own bubble bath, combine two cups of vegetable oil, three tablespoons of liquid shampoo and a few drops of your favorite perfume. Mix the solution with a whisk or put it in the blender for a few seconds. This formula will make your skin soft and save you money to boot!

Smart Reader Solution
I recently received one of those bath puffs and a sample of liquid bath soap in the mail. At first I thought the bath puff was silly but I'm a skinflint, and it was free, so I thought I'd give it a try. I found out that a tiny bit of soap could be used with the puff. It made tons of lather! After the last bit of the free soap was gone I used the bath puff with regular bar soap and found that I could use about half as much soap and get more lather! Those silly little bath puffs will make your soap last

about twice as long!

Add two cups of apple cider vinegar to your bath water. It is great for sore muscles and fatigue. It works better than expensive bath additives.

Smart Reader Solution
Use empty margarine tubs in the shower as a "waste basket." It's a neat place to put soap scraps, razor cartridges and clumps of hair that pile up. It looks neater and saves me from having to reach in later after my shower to throw them away. I poke holes around the bottom to keep water from building up in it and when it is full I toss out the trash.

Save the Skin
Make your own facial cleansing grains by mixing a teaspoon of sugar with your soap lather. This mixture will help remove any dead skin cells. Your skin will feel very soft after using this solution.

Mix baking soda with a small amount of liquid soap to make an inexpensive skin exfoliator (scrub). You simply rub the mixture (I use a washcloth) on whatever part of your body you wish to exfoliate. I also use it on my face but I take extra care not to scrub too hard. Rinse it off with water and your skin will glow.

To dry up a blemish or pimple, dab the area with lemon juice several times a day. Lemon juice works just as good as any of the expensive products available, for a fraction of the cost. Or make a paste of baking soda and peroxide and apply before going to bed.

If you or your teenager tends to have acne, try using salt without iodine in your cooking and on the table. Iodine is essential in the diet, but you will get plenty from other sources. This simple tip could save you tons of money on dermatologists' bills.

Rub about 1 tablespoon of cider vinegar on your hands after a shower, bath or working in the kitchen. It will soften hands very nicely. It's a lot cheaper than hand lotions and not greasy.

Cosmetics
To get every last bit of lotion out of the bottle, put it in the microwave and get it warm, or toss the bottle in your bath water to warm it up; the warm lotion will pour right out.

Refill trail size bottles of lotion, shampoo and other toiletries for traveling. When you return from your vacation save the bottles for your next trip.

To make your razor last longer, store it in the medicine cabinet instead of the shower. When left in the shower, the blade will quickly rust and have to be replaced.

Save used tea bags in the refrigerator, then re-wet with cold water and apply to puffy eyes for about 10 to 15 minutes. This will help reduce the puffiness and relax you!

To get a sharp point on lipstick or eye liner pencils, without much waste, put them in the freezer for about 15 minutes before sharpening.

If you find that you have run out of deodorant you can quickly make a substitute. Mix equal parts of baking soda and cornstarch for a natural deodorant.

Q. Buying a brand name make-up remover and face cleanser at the department store can be very costly. I remember my aunt making a face cleanser out of mayonnaise and some other ingredients. Do you know how to make this? I would like to try something that will not cost me a fortune.

A. Here is a recipe you can make at home. Mix half a cup of mayonnaise with one tablespoon melted butter and the juice of one lemon. Place the face cream in a glass jar and store in the refrigerator. Just take a little out and use it to clean your face and remove any makeup. This will clean and soften your skin. Rinse your face with cold water after cleaning with this homemade formula. One batch will last for a long time.

Hair

Check with local beauty schools and see if they offer night classes to students. At many schools you can get your hair cut for FREE during the class. Either the instructor will cut it as a demonstration to the class or a student will cut it with close supervision by the instructor. Ask about other services such as coloring or permanent waves. Even if they do not offer night classes, the beauty schools will be much more affordable than the local salons.

When you think your shampoo bottle is empty, fill it 1/3 full with water. You'll be amazed at how many more shampoos you'll get!

To save money when coloring your hair, pick a hair color close to your natural color (a shade or two lighter or darker). With a close shade, you won't have to touch up the color as often. When buying hair color, look for a beauty supply store; the price will be much cheaper (usually about half price) than buying it at the drug store.

Although most shampoo bottles instruct you to lather and rinse twice, if you wash your hair daily, you need to only lather once unless your hair is especially dirty.

Kitchen Hair Care

Q. I have heard of people using lemon juice, vinegar, corn meal and even beer or flat champagne on their hair. Do any of these home remedies actually do anything to the hair?

A. Believe it or not, many items from the kitchen are helpful and inexpensive.

Lemon juice brings out the highlights, but also conditions and shines hair. It is typically used by blondes or light brunettes.

Vinegar is a natural conditioner and it will bring out red highlights. Use vinegar as a rinse any time you notice a build-up of any type of hair product.

Corn meal can be used as a dry shampoo. It is especially helpful for people with very oily hair. Just rub it in and brush it out.

Beer conditions the hair. Apply it to wet hair for more body. Just don't let hubby catch you doing it!

Flat Champagne is a very expensive softener and hair rinse.

Skinflint Smile

To get every last bit of toothpaste out of the tube, slip a barrette or an old fashioned clothespin on the tube. Either one works just as good as the plastic keys that you can buy and I'll bet you have one or the other lying around the house.

When the tube of toothpaste is almost empty, place it under warm water for a few minutes to get every last drop out of the tube.

When you think all the toothpaste is used up, cut open the tube; there's enough for several more brushings.

Make your own homemade toothpaste. Take 1 tablespoon baking soda, 1/2 teaspoon salt and 1/4 teaspoon peppermint extract. Mix all ingredients together in a small bowl and use as toothpaste. It works great and even tastes great!

Here's another money saving use for plain old white vinegar. Soak your dentures in white vinegar overnight to clean them. It is much cheaper than the commercial products. You'll pay just a fraction of the cost.

Nail It!
Don't toss away your old toothbrush. Use it as a nail brush to scrub your nails clean. To clean an old toothbrush before using as a nail brush, simply place it in the dishwasher and wash it with a load of dishes.

Before applying nail polish, rub your finger-nails with cotton balls dipped in vinegar. This not only cleans them thoroughly, but will help polish stay on longer.

Don't throw away nail polish that is too thick to use. Place the old bottle in a pan of hot water for a few minutes to restore its smooth consistency.

You don't have to spend extra money on special quick drying nail polish or sprays to make nails dry quickly. Instead, simply dip your painted nails into ice water to make them dry quickly.

Sweet Smell of Perfume
To make your cologne or perfume fragrance last longer, dab a little petroleum jelly on your wrists and mix your perfume or cologne with it. The petroleum jelly will make the fragrance last about twice as long. By doing this, you will be able to put perfume on less often and still enjoy the fragrance all day long.

Don't buy expensive perfumed moisturizers: Instead make your own inexpensive body moisturizer by adding a few drops of your favorite perfume to a small bottle of baby oil.

When wearing a scarf or sweater that will be worn several times before washing, try putting a little perfume on the garment. The fragrance will last much longer when applied to a piece of clothing.

Instead of spraying fragrance directly on

clothing, spray a small amount on your ironing board and the fragrance will transfer to
the clothing.

To make your perfume or cologne last longer,
store it in a dark, cool place. A good place to
store your perfume is in a drawer or even in
the refrigerator.

Shop for perfume bargains after Christmas.
Look for special holiday packages of your
favorite fragrance. Stock up and save at least
50 percent.

Q. My boyfriend gave me perfume that's too
strong. The fragrance is nice, but it is very
overpowering. I've tried just using a very small
amount but it is still too strong. I want to get
to use the perfume. Is there anything I can
do?

A. If your perfume is alcohol based, as many
are, you can dilute it with distilled water. Fill
a small bottle with about two ounces of water
and add perfume one drop at a time. After
each drop, shake the bottle and apply the
mixture to your wrist. Continue adding perfume until the strength seems right to you.
You can also use the scent by adding a few
drops of the perfume to an unscented body
lotion. This should give you a light fragrance
also. If your perfume is oil based, dilute it the
same way using sweet almond oil instead of
water.

7

Shopping on a shoestring

SHOPPING ON A SHOESTRING

CATALOG SHOPPING

When ordering by mail, don't forget to factor the shipping and handling costs into the price of your purchase. You may be able to buy the products cheaper locally. On the other hand, you may not have to pay state sales tax when you shop by mail from another state; so you may be able to at least save the sales tax. It pays to comparison shop!

When you order something through the mail, always write the address and toll-free number of the company on your check. If your order does not arrive within a reasonable amount of time, you can quickly find the number and call to find out what the problem is. It is amazing how catalogs can disappear after you place an order.

You may have seen advertisements in magazines to order catalogs. Most ask you to send a dollar or two for each catalog and another dollar or two for postage and handling. This is a good time to use the toll-free directory (1-800-555-1212) to call the company direct and ask for a catalog. Most companies will gladly send you a FREE catalog.

MAIL ORDER BARGAINS

Q. I just opened a new bank account and

when I received the first statement I was shocked that they charged me $15.00 for an order of 200 checks. I think this is very over-priced. Do I have to order checks from the bank or can I get a printer to make them?

A. There are at least ten different companies that print checks at a fraction of what the banks charge. Most companies charge $4.95 for your first order of 200 personal checks. Other types of checks are also available at discounted prices. To get a catalog and an order form call Current 1-800-533-3973, Checks in the Mail 1-800-733-4443 or Artistic Checks 1-800-224-7621.

Q. Where can I buy discounted magazine subscriptions? I know you can buy oldies from garage sales, read magazines at the library, or borrow from friends; but I am will-ing to pay for home delivery. I know there are companies that offer discounts; but I have not been able to locate them.

A. There are several different companies that offer discounted magazine subscriptions. Two of the best services (with the lowest prices, of course) are Delta Publishing Group, Ltd. 1-800-728-3728 and Below Wholesale Maga-zines 1-800-800-0062. Call and ask for a price listing.

HOW TO HAGGLE

Most people bargain, negotiate or haggle when they buy a car or shop at a garage sale or flea market. But you can and should bargain more often. Here are some tips to help you get the most for your money.

• Be prepared. Know the competitor's comparable prices.

• Smile and be pleasant. Let them know you are ready to buy, but not at the retail price.

• Always deal with someone of authority such as the owner or manager.

• The more you buy, the more leverage you have. For example, if you are remodeling your kitchen, buy all your appliances from the same dealer. He'll be much more willing to give you a discount.

• If you can't get the store to budge on the price, ask them to "throw in" some extras (disks for computers, paper for printers, blank tapes for cassette players, etc.).

• When making a large purchase, always ask for a 5% discount for paying cash. The store has to pay a fee when they accept a credit card. They may be willing to give you a price break to avoid paying the credit card fee.

• Include tax in your offer and be sure you make this clear by saying "tax included."

• Keep in mind that the worst that can happen is the merchant will say no!

TURN YOUR TRASH INTO CASH

Whether you call it a garage, yard or tag sale it is a sure fire way to scrape up a few bucks. Here are some tips to make the most money during your next sale.

When you spring clean this year instead of throwing the junk away, tuck it away in a corner of the garage and start planning for a garage sale. You will be surprised at what people will buy.

Wash, dust and clean everything. Plug in any appliances and have batteries available for any toys or gadgets that require them. You will get more money if you can show it works.

Prepare as much as possible the night before. Shoppers will knock on your door at the crack of dawn. Be ready to start early; but don't let the early birds clean out your merchandise at much lower prices than you have them marked. You can always start to reduce prices in the afternoon if merchandise is not moving.

Make your garage sale a fun place to be. Sell soft drinks, coffee, popcorn or brownies. Set up several extra lawn chairs for shoppers to sit and wait for their friends to finish shopping.

OUTLET SHOPPING
When shopping at an outlet store, always look over potential purchases carefully. Though most outlet clothing is in perfect condition, some items are irregulars. Since many times the items are not marked as irregulars, it pays to examine the item closely. If you are not happy with the quality or find an irregularity, take the item back and ask for a refund or exchange.

Q. I like to shop at outlet stores to save. I'm confused about the different labels on clothes. What is the difference between irregular, seconds and discontinued? What are generally the best buys in outlet stores?

A. Experts say that about 80% of outlet merchandise is first quality, but some of the best buys are slightly flawed. Here's what the labels mean.

Irregular - Items will have tiny imperfections but no serious flaws. For example irregular panty hose can be worn and no one will be able to notice the tiny imperfections.

Seconds - This is flawed merchandise. Generally it is wearable but you need to carefully inspect it to make sure it meets your needs.

Samples - These items have been on display and can be shopworn. The colors may not exactly match coordinating pieces. Sizes and colors will be limited.

Past Season - Last year's styles are this year's best buys. As long as the style is still being worn, past season merchandise can be some of the best bargains.

Discontinued - These items will no longer be manufactured so stores are getting rid of the last pieces. Sizes and colors will usually be limited.

GENERAL SHOPPING TIPS

Don't hesitate to return a product that Doesn't fit your needs. How many times have you bought something then decided it just wasn't quite right? Recently my husband paid $12 for a product to clean the vinyl siding of the house. Later he realized that he could mix up a cleaner for less than one dollar so he decided to return the merchandise and keep his $12. Always save your receipt and return items instead of letting them collect dust. Make better use of your money. Don't hold on to something that you may never use.

If possible, be patient when shopping for anything. Remember that everything goes on sale sooner or later. If you need the item right now, ask the sales clerk or manager when it will go on sale. If they can find that the item will be advertised soon, they may let you buy it at the sale price now. If not, save your receipt and when the item is on sale go back to the store and ask for a refund of the price difference. As long as the sale date and purchase date are reasonably close (within about 6 months) most stores will refund the difference.

When shopping for a specific item (such as a vacuum cleaner or other appliance) find the lowest advertised price. Then take the advertisement with you when shopping because most stores will match competitors advertised prices. Some will even charge 5% to 10% *less than* the advertised price. You may not have to drive from store to store to get the lowest prices.

When shopping, don't be taken in by a promotional gimmick. For instance don't buy a magazine subscription because you wanted the get the "free" sports blooper video or telephone offered with each paid subscription. If you want or need a telephone go and buy one instead of ordering the magazine. The cost of the "free" product is always built into the subscription price and many times the free item is very poor quality. You can find all sorts of sports blooper videos at the library or for sale (usually very cheap) at garage sales.

Q. I swear some retailers mark up merchandise just so they can mark it down and make you think you are getting a bargain. Does anyone ever pay the extremely high retail prices they tag on these items? Am I just imagining this, or do they really mark it up to mark it down?

A. The old retailing trick, tagging the garment with a higher price than anybody ever paid for it and advertising it as a "sale," is alive and well, especially at factory and designer outlet stores. Always comparison shop. Even if it is advertised as 50 percent off you may be able to find it at a lower price in another store.

WHEN TO SHOP
(See Best Buys Calendar page 129)
Buy a new car at the end of the month. Dealers are eager to sell cars before the first of the month, when they have to make interest payments for all cars on the lot. Also, salesmen may be more willing to drop the price at the end of the month if they are just a few sales short of a bonus.

Even consignment and thrift shops have sales. Check with your local stores and find out when they offer the best prices. Some have 3 or 4 big sales each year. Other stores have a certain day of the week (such as Tuesday or Wednesday) that they offer a discount. If you are a senior citizen, ask if they offer a senior's discount.

Shop for major purchases late in the month. You may be better able to negotiate a bargain price on major purchases such as large appliances by shopping just before the end of the month. Many retailers are anxious to meet their monthly sales quotas or goals and some will be willing to lower prices to make an additional sale.

8

Caring for Clothing

CLOTHING

Pack it Away
Q. How can I keep moths out of the clothes that I am getting ready to pack away? I don't like the smell of cedar on my clothes.

A. Scatter dried bay leaves in the boxes and between layers of the clothing you wish to store. The bay leaves will keep the moths away. The bay leaves also do not leave an overpowering odor on the clothes either.

Use inexpensive cedar chips instead of moth-balls to protect your out-of-season clothes. Take an old pair of pantyhose and pour one cup of cedar chips into one leg. Hang the pantyhose with your clothes and it will keep the moths away from your clothes.

After you take your fall sweaters and clothes out of the cedar chest this year re-scent it. All you need to do is rub the inside of the chest with fine sandpaper and vacuum up the dust particles. This will revive the wood's scent, which will help keep the moths out of your clothes.

Shoes
To keep your shoes looking new longer, keep a pair of old slip-ons in the car to change into while driving. This will eliminate the scraped heels and ugly scuff marks you get on your shoes while driving.

Shine your leather or imitation leather shoes with a banana peel. Rub the inside of the peel on your shoes and buff with a soft cloth. The oils in the banana peel will make your shoes last longer.

To keep tennis shoes new looking longer, spray them with starch (regular spray starch used for ironing) before wearing them. The starch will help them stay clean longer. After washing your tennis shoes, apply another coat of spray starch to them as soon as they are dry. If you apply spray starch to your shoes after each washing, you will find that you do not need to wash them as often; which will make them last longer.

When shoelace ends get frayed and hard to lace, try this: Twist the ends tightly (you may have to dampen them a bit), dip them into clear nail polish, and let dry. Your laces will be like new again. To keep the tips on new shoes from breaking off, dip them in clear nail polish and let dry before you wear them.

Don't throw away a fabric softener sheet away after it has been used once. Use it all around the house as an air freshener. To keep your tennis shoes smelling fresh, place a fabric softener sheet into the shoes when you are not wearing them. Toss a fabric softener sheet under your car seat, in your gym bag, or in the bottom or your trash can to keep all these areas smelling fresh.

Sprinkle baking soda in tennis shoes, gym bag or the hamper to keep odors under control. Also use baking soda in the bottom of wardrobe bags where you are storing clothes.

To increase the life of your workout shoes, wear them only for exercise. If your workout shoes get wet, stuff them with rolled up newspapers to help absorb the moisture. When shoes are left wet, they lose their shape and the moisture speeds up the breakdown of shoe materials.

When you buy a new pair of tennis shoes don't automatically throw away the old ones. Instead save them to wear around the house and while working in the yard. This will help make your new shoes stay new looking longer. Keep the oldest pair of shoes in the garage to change into before mowing the lawn or doing any especially dirty yard work.

You'll save money by fixing your old dress shoes instead of buying new ones. While getting shoes repaired, ask what preventative steps you can take to keep your shoes from wearing down and wearing out.

Here's an easy way to dry out wet tennis shoes. Place the shoes on the floor in front of the refrigerator by the grille overnight. The movement from the fan inside will thoroughly dry out the shoes. It works better than tossing them in the dryer. It's quieter and requires no extra electricity.

Q. I recently bought a pair of shoes that seemed to fit just right in the store. I have tried to wear them a couple of times but I end up taking them off because they pinch my toes. Can I take the shoes back even though they are slightly worn? I hate to just push them to the back of my closet. What if I can't find my receipt?

A. Yes you can take the shoes back. These days stores are much more willing to refund your money or exchange merchandise - even if you have used the item slightly. Even without a receipt, most stores will offer you a store credit without a hassle. Large chain stores and department stores have come to realize that writing off a few items is worth the expense because it keeps the customer happy; Which means that you will most likely shop at their store again. You may have more trouble returning items to small stores that are individually owned.

Socks
When the heels and toes of knee high socks are worn, you can cut off the foot portion and make them into ankle socks. Just simply cut the end rounded and sew shut; then you have a bonus pair of ankle socks.

Buy socks in quantity to save money. When you have several pairs of socks that are exactly alike you don't have to discard both socks when one gets a hole in it. Just save the good one and you'll have a mate when another sock gets a hole in it.

Pantyhose

To make pantyhose last longer, add a drop or two of fabric softener to the final rinse. It lubricates the fibers and adds life to your hose.

Put pantyhose in the freezer overnight before wearing them. They will be as tough as nails and resist running.

Q. I spend a big chunk of my clothing budget on panty hose. How can I save money and make them last longer?

A. Buy panty hose with reinforced toes because they are less vulnerable to snags and holes in the toe area.

Buy the largest size will fit properly. The less stress on the fabric, the longer it will last.

Support panty hose will save money even though they cost more. The fabric is much more durable and will stand up to more washings and everyday wear.

Buy panty hose in quantity to save money.

Slightly imperfect panty hose from a national catalog or outlet stores are always a good buy. Chances are you will not be able to spot the imperfection. The hose may be a slightly different shade or a seam in the waistband may not be straight. They will not have any runs in them.

Remove jewelry and make sure your hands are smooth (apply lotion if needed) before you put your panty hose on. Rings and long fingernails can snag or run panty hose.

Some experts recommend rinsing panty hose in beer or salt water. Both seem to coat the fibers and help them last longer. Salt of course is the cheaper of the two. Use about a half cup for each quart of water.

Shirts
When the collar of dress shirts (men's or women's) wear out, remove the collar and turn it over. If you do not sew, take the shirt to a dry cleaner or seamstress and ask them to "turn the collar". Using this trick, you can make your shirts last twice as long.

Cut buttons off worn shirts you are discarding and save them for replacements for others in your closets. Also these soft old shirts make great household rags for dusting and other projects around the house.

Clothes Care and Cleaning

Perspiration odor and stains can be removed from clothes with vinegar. Pour some full strength vinegar on the underarm area before washing.

Add two cups of vinegar to the washing machine when you are washing especially dirty clothes. Not only will the vinegar help clean the clothes, but it will clean soap scum from the washing machine hoses.

The best way to clean a baseball cap is in the dishwasher! Don't waste money buying one of those plastic gadgets to use when washing baseball caps. Just place the ball cap on the top rack of the dishwasher and wash it with your next load of dishes. Promptly take the hat out and reshape it. The cap will look like new. The dishwasher is much more gentle to ball caps than the washing machine.

How to Save on Dry Cleaning

If the three little words DRY CLEAN ONLY make you want to scream, here are some tips to keep the high cost of dry cleaning under control.

Wash delicate clothes by hand or use the gentle cycle of the washing machine. Chances are, most of the things you're dry cleaning are probably hand-washable. Cotton, nylon, silk, ramie and polyester can be washed by hand as long as they are colorfast. To test for colorfastness (the ability to hold dyes without running), blot a white rag dipped in hot water on an inside, unexposed seam of the garment. If the color comes off on to the white rag, you'll have to have it dry-cleaned. Some materials such as acetate and viscose rayon will shrink substantially, so they need to be dry-cleaned.

Dry-clean less frequently. After each wearing, remove any soil from jackets or coats by brushing with a soft bristled brush. Let wrinkles smooth out by allowing them to hang for a few days. Many times a skirt or pair or suit pants may not need to be dry cleaned; they just need the wrinkles ironed out.

Always dry clean the entire suit. Don't be tempted to just have the pants or skirt cleaned and wait until next time to clean the jacket. Dry cleaning can slightly change (or fade) the color of your garments, so over time your suit may not be the exact color.

Point out any stains and let your cleaner know exactly what the stain is. Dry cleaners are very proficient at removing stains; but once the garment is cleaned the stain will be harder to remove and may be permanent.

Buy clothes from the dry cleaner. Once a year many dry cleaners will sell off the clothes that have not been picked up. Most will sell them for the price of the cleaning! I picked up a beautiful blazer and several nice dresses for just a few dollars.

Tiny Tightwads
Play clothes for little girls cost more than similar items in the boys department. For casual pants and tops, buy your daughter's play clothes in the boys' department. Women can also buy tee shirts, jackets and shorts cheaper in the men's department.

To make children's jeans last longer, iron or sew patches on the inside of the jeans before they wear them. Then when they fall down on their knees, the jeans won't rip as easily. Use the largest size patch that will fit inside for the most protection.

Oh the Smell!
Don't throw away the fragrance strips from magazines, instead place them in your drawers to make your clothes smell nice.

You can make your own inexpensive sachets to keep your closets and drawers smelling fresh. Save an old pair of pantyhose. Cut off the legs and fill them with your favorite potpourri. Tie the end shut to hold the potpourri inside. Place them on your closet shelves, in the back of drawers or any place you want to add a little fragrance.

Pour baking soda into old socks or knee high hose and put in smelly sneakers or other shoes to keep them fresh smelling. This works better than sprinkling baking soda or powder directly into the shoes, since you can reuse the sock or hose many times.

Miscellany

To help remove crease line when lowering a hem, wet a piece of cloth with plain white vinegar. Rub it across the hem line then iron the hem dry (adjust iron setting according to material).

Don't buy special skirt hangers. Clothespins will hold skirts on a regular hanger.

When buying clothes, look for items that can worn year round. You can easily add a sweater or jacket during the cold winter months. Look for versatile fabrics like rayon and cotton/wool blends that can be layered in the winter, but will stay cool in the summer.

Q. What can be used as protection for new fabric bags? A new fabric bag (purse) quickly becomes dirty and has to be replaced. Is there anything that can be sprayed on to the bag?

A. Spray a light coating of spray starch to fabric purses or canvas shoes. The starch will keep the fabric looking newer longer. After you wash fabric purses or shoes, apply another coat of spray starch after the fabric dries.

9

Keep
it
Clean

Cleaning Tips

Dusting
To keep lint off glass top tables, wash them in a solution of warm water and fabric softener. Add one capful of liquid fabric softener to one quart of warm water. The fabric softener will clean the glass and will help keep lint from gathering on the glass.

Grab a handful of used dryer sheets when dusting furniture. They leave a nice shine but the dust clings to them instead of just being moved around. Another bonus is no furniture polish build-up.

Don't throw away worn out or odd socks that have lost their mate; Instead use them to dust and polish furniture. Socks are perfect to place over your hands to dust the hard to reach areas. Put a little homemade furniture polish on the sock and see how fast and easy you can get the dusting finished.

Place a sock over a yard stick (use a rubber band to hold the sock in place) to reach hard to dust spots. Use the yard stick to remove all the dust bunnies between the refrigerator and the cabinets. The yard stick is also very handy to get cob webs down from the ceiling. You can buy an expensive mop type duster, but a homemade yard stick duster works just as good.

Good weather sealing around doors and windows not only saves money on heating and cooling, but also cuts down dusting dramatically.

Q. Please answer the age old question: Should I vacuum or dust first? I have tried it both ways and I can't seem to come to a conclusion.

A. Vacuum carpets and rugs first, then wait a few minutes (or do another chore) before dusting. After vacuuming the dust particles are in the air from the vacuum cleaner's beaters. If you wait for this dust to settle your furniture will not have to be dusted twice. You'll save time and use less furniture polish.

Here's an inexpensive "recipe" for homemade furniture polish. It works like a charm.

To make your own furniture polish, mix one part lemon juice (fresh or bottled) with two parts vegetable oil. Store the homemade polish in a clean plastic bottle. Label it with a black marker so you (and everyone else in the house) will know what's inside. Use an old rag to polish your wood furniture. Simply rub in a small amount of the polish. It will clean your wood furniture and make your it shine. Save the same old rag (or old sock) to use each week just for dusting; place it in a plastic bag and close the top, this way you will only have to add a very small amount of furniture polish each week since the rag will stay moist.

Vacuum
To keep your vacuum cleaner smelling fresh, put several cloves into the vacuum cleaner bag. The cloves also add a fresh clean scent to the air.

To speed cleaning time, use a long extension cord with your vacuum cleaner. Then you don't have to take time to unplug the cord and find a new outlet. You will be surprised how much faster you finish vacuuming.

Floors
To make your mops and brooms last longer, store them off the floor. Hang them on nails in the garage or utility room.

The best cleaner for ceramic tile floors or unwaxed linoleum is vinegar. Use about 1/2 cup white vinegar to 1/2 bucket of warm water. This solution works better than any store bought floor cleaning product. It makes the floors sparkle and shine.

Don't throw away odd socks or socks with holes in them. Use them to make a skinflint mop. Tie several socks to a mop or broom handle and use as a regular mop. White cotton socks work best for this project. By the time the "sock mop" wears out, you'll probably have plenty more socks to make a new one.

Q. How can I remove black scuff marks on vinyl floors?

A. To remove black scuff marks on vinyl or linoleum floors, use regular white toothpaste. Rub the paste into the black mark and wipe it away with a damp cloth. If the scuff marks are especially tough, add a little baking soda to the toothpaste and they should come right off.

Carpet
Stubborn candle wax can be removed from linens or carpeting by pressing a warm (not hot) iron over a paper towel directly on the spot. Continue to iron until the wax melts and is absorbed into the paper towel.

To keep your carpet looking like new, vacuum the traffic areas very often. Take your time and slowly run the vacuum cleaner over the carpet. Also, be sure to wipe the bristles clean on your vacuum cleaner every couple of weeks. This will also help keep your carpet new looking longer.

To prevent furniture legs staining your carpet when you shampoo it, place clear plastic bags (the ones from newspapers work great) over the legs before shampooing the carpet.

Windows
When washing windows, you can use old newspapers instead of paper towels or rags.

The newspapers are inexpensive and won't leave lint on the windows.

Wash windows with automotive windshield cleaner. It does not streak and leaves a beautiful shine. You get so much more for your money when you buy a large jug of windshield cleaner instead of a small bottle of window cleaner.

Use old panty hose or old socks to wash windows. Both work great and won't leave lint.

My favorite way to clean windows is to dip old newspapers (black and white pages only) into a solution of half vinegar and half water. Wipe the glass with the wet newspapers until the glass is almost dry, then shine with dry newspapers or a soft cloth (like an old diaper or thin towel). The combination of vinegar and newspapers can't be beat and the price can't be beat either!

To remove small scratches in glass and mirrors, rub the scratches with white toothpaste. This is especially helpful for glass top tables.

Q. I always get streaks when I wash my windows. I also end up with lint from my paper towels on the windows. What am I doing wrong?

A. Never wash windows when the sun is shining on them; the sun will cause windows to streak. Use a cheap chamois, old pantyhose, or old crumpled newspapers to wipe with. All of these are inexpensive and will not leave lint on your windows. I personally use old newspapers. I think they work best and they really seem to make the windows shine. When washing windows, use up-and-down strokes on one side of the glass and use side-to-side strokes on the other. This way you can see which side needs extra polishing.

Kitchen
Instead of using steel wool pads, use a loofah sponge. To make a large loofah sponge into manageable pieces to work with, cut it lengthwise, then cut each half into six or eight pieces. These are much gentler to the hands than steel wool and they won't rust.

Instead of throwing away a sponge that has a stale odor, simply toss it in the dishwasher and wash it with the next load of dishes. It will come out clean and fresh smelling.

Wash old toothbrushes (used for cleaning) and combs in the dishwasher. It gets them really clean without scrubbing.

When cleaning stainless steel counter tops, ranges or sinks, use club soda. It cleans like a charm and dries to a gleam without streaks or spots. Don't throw away flat club soda; even flat it still works to clean stainless steel.

Here's a tip for cleaning stainless steel sinks. When you change the baking soda in the refrigerator (to keep odors under control) spread the old baking soda over the damp sink. It will cling to the sides and bottom. Let it sit for at least one hour. It can stay on longer with no harm. Use a sponge to wipe it around as you rinse thoroughly. The sink will be clean with no spots. The baking soda goes down the drain to help the pipes stay clean smelling.

To keep copper items looking new, wet the copper and sprinkle salt on it. Then rub to a shine with a lemon slice. Rinse, and the copper will shine like new.

Q. I have stainless steel sinks and even when they are clean they look dirty because they always seem to have soap or water spots. I have used all kinds of different cleaning products. Any inexpensive suggestions would help.

A. A light coating of mineral oil or baby oil will help prevent soap and water spots on stainless steel sinks. Wash and dry the sinks before applying the oil.

Q. Can you give me some suggestions how to remove grease from painted walls? I would like to find an inexpensive formula for this tough job.

A. Here's the best homemade formula I have

found for grease removal. Combine 1 cup household ammonia, 1/4 cup baking soda or Borax, and 1/2 cup white vinegar. Mix in a bucket with 1 gallon warm water. Always wash walls from the bottom up, as dirty water dripping down the wall can leave streaks that are nearly impossible to remove. Here's another tip for keeping walls cleaner. I have found that a coat or two of white shellac right around the switch plates on the wall makes that area very easy to clean. You can quickly wipe away greasy fingerprints, dirt or grime with a damp sponge.

Bathroom
To make a container for your toilet brush, cut off the top 1/3 of a plastic 1/2 gallon milk container. You can even leave the handle on it to make it easy to carry from one bathroom to another.

Instead of buying expensive lime removers for the toilet and other bathroom fixtures, try hydrogen peroxide first. It can do the job for a fraction of the price.

To clean really stubborn hard water rings in the toilet bowl, pour some cola into the bowl and let it sit for one hour. You can use any brand of cola (even flat cola), but it must be cola, not lemon-lime or any other flavor.

For cleaning the toilet, try denture cleanser tablets! Just drop one in the bowl and let it bubble away the stains. If you have a build up, you will need to swish a toilet brush around to loosen the grime; but if you do this regularly, you won't even have to scrub. It is much cheaper than buying those blue toilet bowl cleaners that go into the tank.

Smart Reader Solution
To get nasty soap scum and dirt off your tub or shower, put a little baby oil in a spray bottle and mix with water. Spray the mixture on a section and wipe off with a sponge. I've never found a cleaner (at any price) that gets soap scum off easier. When I'm done, I just go over once with a disinfectant cleaner to make sure all the germs are killed! This saves money (baby oil is cheap) and it saves time too!

Prevent mildew on a plastic shower curtain by soaking it in warm saltwater before hanging.

Q. How can I remove really stubborn bathtub decals? I just bought an older house and the decals have probably been on the tub for many years.

A. First try full-strength vinegar. Pour the vinegar around the edges of the decal and let it soak for 30 minutes. This should loosen them so you can pull them off. If the vinegar does not work, try nail polish remover. Apply it around the edge of the decals and pull them up. Use a little more nail polish remover or vinegar to clean off any remaining sticky residue. Be sure to rinse away the finger nail polish remover or vinegar with soapy water.

To clean a bathroom, don't dilute your cleaner in a bucket of water. Instead, dilute a smaller amount into a spray bottle. Spray one surface at a time and wipe with a damp cloth. Less mess and cheaper!

Use rubbing alcohol (70% isopropyl) in a spray bottle for bathroom fixtures. It cleans perfectly with no abrasive action. It is a natural cleaner that will not build up on fixtures or mirrors.

To clean that nasty scum off your permanent shower heads, take a little plastic bag and fill it half full of vinegar. Tape it on your shower head so that the shower head is immersed in the vinegar. Wait 1/2 hour to 1 hour depending on how bad the build up is. Wipe it off and it should be as clean as new.

To keep a bathroom mirror from fogging up, rub a bit of moistened soap on to the mirror, then wipe it off with a towel. You can use bar soap lather or creamy soft soap to do the trick. The area where soap was applied will stay fog-free for several weeks, no matter how steamy the bathroom gets.

Clean scum and water residue from tub and sink drains with about 1/2 cup baking soda and about 1 cup vinegar; This mixture will also take away any bad odors in the drains. Just pour the baking soda down follow it with the vinegar, let it sit for a few minutes and flush with water.

Instead of buying expensive mildew remover, try using rubbing alcohol. It works great at removing mildew and other stains from the silicone caulking around the tub.

For really tough jobs such as cleaning ceramic tiles, radiators, air vents or dirty shower stalls, use 1/4 cup baking soda in a gallon of very warm water with 1/2 cup vinegar and 1 cup clear ammonia. Wear rubber gloves and clean in a well-ventilated area.

Scrub porcelain enamel bath tubs and sinks with a solution of hot water and a few drops of liquid dishwashing detergent. The mixture will easily clean the fixtures without scratching the shiny finish.

To remove mold and mildew from shower curtains, spray a solution of half vinegar and half water on the curtains and let it soak for a few minutes.

For a shiny porcelain white sink, cover the sink with paper towels saturated in bleach. Let stand for 30 minutes; then rinse thoroughly with cool water. The bleach will also remove many stubborn stains without scrubbing.

Q. I usually replace my shower curtain when it gets too dirty. I think they are very hard to clean. Is there any way to wash a shower curtain that does not include scrubbing?

A. The easiest way to get a shower curtain really clean is to wash it in the washing machine. Fill the washing machine with warm water and two or three dirty towels (we all have plenty). Add 1/2 cup of laundry detergent and 1/2 cup of baking soda. Then wash adding 1 cup white vinegar to the rinse cycle. Pull the shower curtain out after the rinse cycle, then let the towels continue through the spin dry cycle. Hang the shower curtain back up immediately and the wrinkles will disappear as the curtain dries. This is so easy, you won't be tempted to throw it away when it gets dirty.

To clean the white grout in the bathroom, dip an old toothbrush or nail brush (reserved only for this purpose) into full strength bleach and scrub away the dirt and mildew.

Soap Solutions
To keep soap bars from melting into a soggy mess, place a sponge under the bar of soap. Then use the sponge to wash with. This will help keep the area neat and you will actually use most of the melted soap instead of washing the soapy mess down the drain.

Instead of throwing away the end pieces of soap, make soap on a rope. Take an old pair of pantyhose and place the small pieces inside. The soap on a rope will stretch to any length you want.

When the bar of soap gets too small to handle, don't throw it away. You can make it into inexpensive soft soap for filling hand soap dispensers. You can either melt the soap in hot water or blend the soap pieces in the blender to make soft soap.

If you notice that your bar of soap seems to have lost it suds, prick the bar with a straight pin or a fork and you should be able to get much more lather out of the bar.

Open bars of soap as soon as you buy them. They will harden and last longer. Place the open bars in drawers to make your clothes smell fresh.

Instead of buying expensive liquid soaps for hand washing, fill your pump dispensers with the least expensive shampoo you can find. The shampoo works great and it is very gentle to your hands.

Save time and money by using the cheapest brand if dishwashing detergent. Add three tablespoons of vinegar to your bottle of liquid dishwashing soap. Shake the bottle to mix the liquids. This tip is so handy because it makes the soap mild on your hands and the soap lasts longer. The best part is it makes your dishes, counter tops and cabinets shine, shine, shine!

Most household detergents are highly concentrated. Experiment with your favorite brand, you can usually use 1/2-3/4 of the suggested amount and still do the job right.

Cleanser (scouring powder) is often wasted because the containers have too many or large holes. To keep the cleanser from coming out too fast, cover half of the holes with masking tape. You will find that you use less cleanser to do the job. This especially works helpful when children clean their own bathrooms!

Misc. Cleaning
To clean a chandelier or glass light fixture all you need is a spray bottle filled with rubbing alcohol, an umbrella and some plastic bags. Cover the light bulbs with plastic bags to keep them dry. I use the plastic bags from throw away newspapers. Hang the umbrella from the light to catch the alcohol drips. Spray the lighting fixture clean with full strength rubbing alcohol. Just let the alcohol drip dry. Your light fixture will dry clean. No scrubbing required!

When cleaning around the house, use a plastic wastebasket as a scrub pail. The wastebasket gets washed out without any extra effort and you don't have to spend money on an extra plastic bucket.

Q. How can I clean my mattress and box springs? I'm not sure what I should use to get it clean.

A. Here's an easy, inexpensive way to clean soiled mattresses or box springs: Use a solution of a quarter cup of liquid dishwashing detergent and one cup warm water. Whip the solution into a high foam with an egg beater. Apply the foam to the mattress or box springs with a stiff brush, working on a small area at a time. Use a damp sponge to remove any soap residue. To speed drying, use an electric fan.

Q. How can I eliminate cigarette smoke in a room? I frequently have guests to my house that smoke, after they leave, I spray air freshener to try to get rid of the smoke and odor. I can still see the smoke and smell the air freshener and cigarette odor.

A. The best (and cheapest) way I have found to eliminate cigarette smoke in a room, is to soak a towel in water, wring it out completely and swish it around the room. This is a quick way to get rid of the smoke. To remove the cigarette odor, sprinkle baking soda on the carpet, let it soak for 30 minutes, then vacuum.

Tiny Tightwads

To clean a child's favorite stuffed animal, rub in a little corn starch and let it soak in for a few minutes. Brush the corn starch off with a toothbrush or other soft brush and toss the stuffed animal into the dryer on low or no heat for a couple of minutes.

To remove greasy finger marks from cloth book covers or cloth wall coverings, rub the marks with stale bread. Brush any crumbs away with an old soft bristled toothbrush.

Toothpaste works wonders removing crayon marks from painted walls. Just scrub crayon drawings with toothpaste, then rinse and wipe dry. This works well on enamel paints as well as flat paints.

Freshen the Air

Revive old room deodorizers by soaking the inner absorbent pad in pine cleaner.

Instead of expensive air fresheners, take your favorite perfume and spray a little on a cotton ball and wipe it on light bulbs around the house. When you turn lights on, the heat releases the scent.

Use plastic film canisters to make small air fresheners. Fill canisters with baking soda and poke a few holes in the lids. These air fresheners are perfect in drawers, cabinets, luggage and trash cans. Replace the baking soda as needed.

Here's an easy way to make your own room air freshener. Just cut an orange, grapefruit, lemon or lime in half, remove the pulp, then fill the shell with salt. This skinflint air freshener will provide a pleasant aromatic scent anywhere in your home. I keep one under the kitchen and bathroom sinks. They really do work wonders! When you make fresh juice, save the rinds in the freezer until you need to make a new air freshener.

Jewelry/Silver
White toothpaste is an inexpensive jewelry cleaner. It will make your gold or silver jewelry sparkle. You can use an old toothbrush to polish the jewelry clean.

Place a piece of white chalk in your silver chest or jewelry box to absorb moisture and prevent tarnishing of silverware or jewelry.

You can clean costume jewelry by putting it in a bowl and pouring rubbing alcohol over it. Let it stand a few minutes and all the tarnish will come off. After wiping, the jewelry will look like new.

Q. How can I clean tarnished sterling silver? I know the silver pieces are not worth much money but they belonged to my great-grandmother, so they are priceless to me.

A. Make up a solution of 1/2 cup clear house-hold ammonia, 1/2 cup warm water, and 1 tablespoon of a mild liquid detergent. Depending on how tarnished the silver is, soak it in the solution for up to an hour. Rinse under warm tap water until all the ammonia solution is removed. Place the silver pieces on a clean towel and pat dry. Silver tarnishes when it is exposed to air. To keep your silver from tarnishing as often, store it in a cloth pouch or wrap it in tissue paper.

Hands Down
Use baking soda as a hand cleaner. After working in the yard, sprinkle it onto wet hands and rub. Rinse and dry. It will remove the dirt and grime in no time flat.

To make your own inexpensive hand cleaner, mix 1/2 cup powdered laundry detergent and 1/2 cup corn meal. Store the mixture in a covered jar.

Furniture
To clean white marks off wood tables, use mayonnaise! Just rub it in the mayonnaise and wipe it off, and the marks should be gone!

Use pantyhose as a quick and easy way to remove lint from upholstered furniture. Panty hose works just as good as a lint brush and it is much easier than getting out the vacuum cleaner!

Here is a good solution for cleaning wood paneling. It's easy on the hands and it leaves a nice finish on paneling. Mix four tablespoons of vinegar, two tablespoons of olive oil and one pint of warm water.

10

Tiny Tightwads

TINY TIGHTWADS

Bath Time

Don't throw away small slivers of soap. Put the small pieces of soap into an old white sock and tie up the open end. Most children prefer this over a bar of soap since it will not slip from their hands.

Little children and playful cats or dogs love to watch a roll of toilet tissue spin off the roll. To prevent roll-offs, before inserting the new roll of tissue on the holder, squeeze the roll together so the cardboard tube is no longer round. This will also keep everyone in the house from pulling off too much paper.

Bath time sponges for kids in animal and other shapes are at least twice the price of regular sponges. Buy inexpensive foam sponges and cut your own shapes. For more cheap bath time fun, add a drop or two of food coloring to the water. You can make the tub a blue ocean, green lake or pink paradise.

Low Cost Fun

Make inexpensive finger-paints for children by mixing two cups of cold water and one quarter cup of cornstarch, then boil the liquid until thick. Pour into smaller containers (baby food jars work great) and color with food colorings. Add a drop of liquid dishwashing detergent to make clean-up easy. Let the paints cool to room temperature before using.

To get a sharp point on crayons without much waste, put them in the freezer for about 15 minutes before sharpening.

Q. My grandchildren will be visiting soon. Can you please print the recipe for making your own dough for children to play with?

A. This is a fun project to make and play with. Here's what you'll need: 1 cup flour, 1/2 cup salt, 2 tablespoons cream of tartar, 1 cup water and 1 tablespoon cooking oil. Mix ingredients and cook over medium heat until it becomes the consistency of dough. Let it cool and add a few drops of food coloring if desired. Your grandchildren will have many hours of inexpensive fun. This is always a great rainy day project.

Save plastic strawberry baskets and use them to entertain youngsters. Dip them in soapy water, then wave them through the air. They will make clouds of bubbles.

Smart Reader Solution
Over the years the best and cheapest glue I have been able to find is a cold boiled potato. Break the potato in two pieces (instead of cutting) and rub on paper as you would any regular glue. I have used this type of glue in my Bible and Sunday school classes for many years. I use it at home to paste recipes into my recipe book and it has held my pictures in

a scrapbook for over 50 years! I am eighty-eight years old. My mother taught me this trick.

Smart Reader Solution
I save computer paper that has been used on one side to donate to my daughter's day care center. They use the paper to make all sorts of drawings, paintings an other creative things. The best thing about doing this is it helps to keep my day care prices from going up. They also ask parents to save all sorts of things such as toilet paper tubes, egg cartons, pieces of cardboard and foam trays to mention a few. They use these for various craft products. I like it that they are teaching the children to have fun with simple things.

When you take your children to the library, take all the library cards out of the books and put them in a plastic bag. Hang the plastic bag near your calendar. Make a note on the calendar when the books are due so you can make sure they are returned without a fine.

Toys
Start an annual toy swap party with other families. Swap the toys your kids have out-grown or are tired of and get some "new" toys.

Use wood building blocks (alphabet block toys) to replace broken or lost knobs on children's furniture. Take a long screw and simply screw the alphabet block into the drawer. To personalize the furniture, use the child's initials.

Give stuffed animals a dry bath by sprinkling them with baking soda. Let them sit for 15 minutes, then brush clean or toss in the dryer with no heat for a few minutes.

Save the hangers that socks come on and use them as hangers for doll clothes. They work perfect.

Smart Reader Solution
I have found a very inexpensive toy to entertain my grandchildren when they visit. I save a few plastic egg cartons. They use one as a cash register to play store. I fill it pennies and play money. I have another filled with cheap costume jewelry. Either one of these will keep them entertained for hours.

Batteries Not Included!
Here are some tips to help you get the most for your money when buying batteries.

When you shop for batteries, always check for expiration dates. Look for batteries that expire as far into the future as possible. If the store is properly rotates merchandise, the newest batteries will be at the back of the shelf.

Batteries will last longer if you store them in the refrigerator. Batteries need to stay dry, so when storing batteries in the refrigerator keep them in a zip-tight (airtight) bag or container. Let the batteries reach room temperature before using them.

To prevent corrosion, remove batteries from devices that won't be used for a long time.

To get the most use out of batteries, don't mix old and new batteries, or different types of batteries in the same device.

Before using batteries, make sure the terminals are clean. When in doubt, clean them with a dry towel or pencil eraser.

Rechargeable batteries are a great buy because, over time, they pay for themselves (batteries and recharger).

Recharge batteries only in chargers (same brand and type) made especially for them.

When shopping for a recharger, look for one that won't overcharge if left plugged in too long. Also look for rechargeables that offer a lifetime warranty to replace used batteries that will no longer hold a charge.

Food for the Wee Ones
Make your own baby food. Puree home cooked foods in a food processor or blender, and freeze individual portions in an ice cube tray. Transfer the baby food cubes into freezer bags.

Buy small glass or plastic bottled drinks on sale. Refill the bottles with inexpensive lemonade or juice made from concentrate. The glass or plastic bottles usually hold a larger amount than the little boxes of juice and even your teenagers will like drinking them.

Here's a way to save on clean-ups. Put a marshmallow inside the empty ice cream cone before you add ice cream. It will eliminate the messy drips through the bottom.

Smart Reader Solution
Kids love ice cream treats. They are very expensive at the grocery store. To save money make your own. Buy a cheap gallon of ice cream and some cones. Dip the ice cream into the cones and let them freeze hard. You can even dip them in chocolate for an extra special treat. By making a bunch of them at one time it makes it easy for them to get a treat without having to stop and dip ice cream for them.

Kids are Messy! (Cleaning Tips)
Q. How can I remove crayon marks from the walls? My three year old has left several pieces of art around the house that I would like to remove. Some of the drawings are on painted walls and a few are on wallpaper.

A. On painted walls (especially white walls) regular white toothpaste usually works great. Rub a dab of toothpaste on the crayon marks and wash away with warm water. For large drawings and wallpaper, you may want to try removing the crayons with a hair dryer. Use a hair dryer set on low to warm the marks for a few seconds, then wipe the area clean with a damp cloth.

To clean scuff marks or crayon drawings off painted walls, mix four tablespoons of baking soda with one quart of warm water.

A child sized shovel makes a perfect dust pan! It holds more dirt and dust and the longer handle makes it less strenuous on the back.

Thrifty Kids
Put your children in charge of saving aluminum cans and glass bottles for deposits. Let them make the returns and keep the money.

Take your kids to garage sales and teach them how to bargain for what they want to buy.

Give your children a list of chores to complete before you give them their allowance. This will help them learn the concept of earning money.

Collect sticks and branches that fall into your yard throughout the year, store them in a dry place, and burn during winter instead of expensive store-bought kindling. This is a fun chore to delegate to your children. Save paper bags to collect the sticks; then you can light the bag to get the fire started.

Clothes
Recycle worn winter pajamas into summer sleep wear by cutting off legs and sleeves.

Buy clothes for children in durable fabrics that will stand up to a lot of wear. Avoid thin, flimsy fabrics and shirts with novelty items glued on that will come off in the washing machine.

Store kid's clothes in labeled boxes to keep them organized. This makes it easy to pass them down to younger siblings.

Choose clothes with an elastic waist or without a defined waistline which will grow with the child.

Have a neighborhood annual garage sale; but even before the garage sale, have an annual swap meet for clothing. Everyone brings the clothes that their family members no longer wears. It is fun to see a variety of neighborhood children getting good use out of the clothes that your children can no longer wear. Kids enjoy picking out their "new" clothes. It is a great way to save money. All of the children (and parents of course!) will look forward to the annual event.

See Ya' in the Funny Papers!
Instead of buying expensive wrapping paper

for my grandchildren's gifts, I wrap their gifts in the Sunday comics and tie them with colorful ribbon. The children enjoy the festive wrapping as much as they would expensive gift paper and I am able to use the money I save to buy a nicer gift for the child. Paper grocery bags are used as the outside wrapping on gifts I send to out-of-town grandchildren. I feel good about my recycling efforts, and I hope that my children and grandchildren will learn through my example that recycling is an acceptable and necessary practice to preserve the earth's resources.

Back to School Supplies:
Stock up on paper, pencils and other supplies that your children will need for the school year during the back to school sales. Look for the advertisements and buy the limit of the "door buster" items. Discount, grocery and drug stores will all have back to school sales; shop them all and stock up on the items they are selling cheap to get you in the store.

Wait to buy special supplies until your child's teacher requests that they bring them in. Many schools will send a "required list of supplies" that each child is "required" to buy. Some of these lists include everything from a slide rule to colored glue and stickers! If a teacher is planning a special project that requires additional supplies, she will let the students know when they are required to bring them in. If you buy all the products on the list you will spend a fortune and chances are good that many of the supplies will not be used or the teacher will get them donated by a local business.

Look for good buys on office supplies that you use around the house. Many times index cards, envelopes and writing paper go on sale during the back to school blitz. Stock up!

Keep all the school supplies in a special drawer or other storage space. Before buying anything new check to see if you already have it on hand.

Back to School Clothes Tips:
Just like school supplies, many stores will have bargain prices on socks and underwear during the back to school season. Stock up on socks and underwear for the *entire family* during the terrific back to school sales.

If you have several small children, buy basics that can be passed down to either sex. Red and blue shorts or tee shirts are perfect for boys or girls. To make a hand-me down from an older brother look more feminine, sew some lace on the collar, pocket or around the sleeves.

Older children will need to have clothes like their peers to help them fit in. Self esteem is very important to preteens and teenagers;

they need to pick out their own clothes. At this age it is a good idea to give them a certain amount of money and let them pick out exactly what they want to wear. Try not to be critical of their choices (as long as the clothes are modest and socially acceptable). Let your children learn to shop and stay within a budget.

Look for tee shirts, shorts, jackets and other accessories for girls and young women in the boy's and men's departments. Almost always these items will be much cheaper than buying a similar item on the girls or teens department.

Back to School (or work) Lunch Tips:
Prepackaged individual bags of crackers, chips or cookies are very expensive per ounce. Buy potato chips, cookies and other lunch goodies in large bags or boxes and repackage into just the right amount for your child.

Plastic bags used for chips and cookies can be used several times. Have your child bring home their lunch box (or bag) with the baggies inside so you can decide whether to use them again or toss them.

Instead of buying expensive drink boxes for lunches, put their favorite drink into a plastic container with a lid. (Some margarine tubs are perfect for a drinking glass, since they are tall and slim.) Freeze the drink (noncarbonated) to keep it cold until lunch time.

To make the perfect peanut butter and jelly sandwich spread peanut butter on both sides of the bread, then put the jelly in the middle of the peanut butter. This will keep the bread from getting soggy.

Mornings are hectic enough, make lunches the night before. Older children can make their own lunches. Smaller children can help. You can even package enough chips, cookies, carrot sticks or whatever for the whole week and then just make a sandwich the night before.

When baking cupcakes for school lunches don't frost the top; instead cut open the cake and put the frosting in the middle. It will be easy to eat, without the frosting sticking to the wrapping.

Back to School Tips:
With school starting most children will also begin after school activities such as sports or other lessons. Make friends with the other moms that go to the same events; work out a car pool schedule to give you more time and save gas.

If your children are too old for a day care and still too young to be left alone, find a neighborhood teenager to baby-sit after school. The teen will appreciate the money and you will spend less than a day care but still get the security from having someone watch your children.

Kids will need a haircut before starting school; check out a book or video from the library on haircutting and learn to cut their hair. The current short hair styles for boys are especially easy to cut. Buy a few tools, and save quite a bit of money. Even if you do not feel confident doing a complete haircut, you can trim the bangs out of your kids eyes to extend the time between haircuts.

If you have not had your child's eyes checked in a few years call around to local eye clinics and see if any offer free vision testing for school age children. Many clinics offer to a once a year free vision screening during the back to school season.

Don't buy expensive book covers. Look around the house for something to use as a book cover. Use paper grocery bags, leftover wallpaper or even old posters to make book covers. The kids will love their "designer" book covers.

11

Pets & Pests

PETS/PESTS

PETS

To keep ants out of your pet's food, place the food dish in a larger bowl filled with water. This way, your pet will have plenty of water and the ants can't get to their food.

To save money on dog or cat food switch from wet food to dry food. When you buy wet food you are paying extra for water and more packaging.

Save money and preserve your pet's health by not overfeeding him or her. If you can't feel the ribs easily, reduce his or her food a little bit at each meal. Ask you veterinarian approximately how much your pet should weigh.

Wash and save the plastic trays that comes with meat or produce and use them to feed your pets. When the tray gets grungy, just toss away the old one and use a "new" one.

When you open a can of tuna fish, don't pour the juice (water or oil) off the tuna down the drain; instead pour it over your cat's food. He will love the added flavor.

Resist the temptation to stock up on dry pet food. Even with proper storage, the vitamins and minerals in the food deteriorate after a few months and there is a good chance the food will become moldy. Buy only what your pet will eat within a couple of weeks.

Q. What's the best soap or shampoo for cleaning dogs? There are plenty of high priced soaps and shampoos, but what's the most economical?

A. During bath time you can use any inexpensive shampoo or liquid soap to bath your cat or dog. Shop for inexpensive "people" shampoo at a discount drug store to use on your pets. If you clip coupons you can buy shampoo for much less than one dollar per bottle. I buy an inexpensive shampoo and conditioner in one, which helps to eliminate tangles and make her coat soft. If your pet has fleas, use dandruff shampoo to bathe her. Look for an inexpensive brand or even a store brand of dandruff shampoo.

After you dry your pet, sprinkle some baking soda on her to keep her smelling clean and fresh between baths.

When giving your dog a bath add a little vinegar to the rinse water to minimize soap film. Rinse your pet thoroughly.

To get rid of fleas, crush a clove if garlic or mix a tablespoon of yeast into cat's or dog's food. It will keep fleas away and make her coat shiny. Or try adding a few drops of vinegar to your pet's water bowl. This trick can also get rid of fleas and ticks.

Use old socks to make an inexpensive cat toy. To make the toy, tie off the toe end and pour a little catnip into the sock. Tie the other end closed. Your kitty will enjoy her soft toy.

Make an inexpensive cat scratching post by stapling a carpet remnant onto a log. You can then nail the log to a wooden base. Your cat will enjoy playing with this for hours and hopefully she won't claw the furniture.

Instead of buying an expensive cat litter with a built in deodorizer; buy an inexpensive brand of cat litter and add baking soda to the bottom of the cat litter tray to absorb more odors.

To save money adopt a pet from a local animal shelter. Even if they charge a small adoption fee, you'll still save money. Many shelters offer reduced fees on basic veterinary care and often shots and neutering or spaying is included in the adoption fee. If you are searching for a particular breed ask the animal shelter if they will call you when one is available for adoption.

Newspapers are great for picking up large spills and pet "accidents" and of course they work great for washing windows. Recycle any extra newspapers that you can't use around the house.

It you have a cat that goes crazy for catnip, you can save money by growing your own catnip. One packet of seeds will harvest enough catnip for the year. It is very easy to grow. You can expect to get three or more cuttings. Just dry the cuttings and place a small amount into an old sock and your cat will have hours of fun.

Never buy dog collars. Instead go to garage sales, thrift stores and flea markets; they always have belts. Buy a belt and cut it to the correct size and punch holes in it. It works great and it saves money.

PESTS

Those Annoying Ants

If you can't seem to win the battle with ants; here are some low cost solutions.

Ant hills (outside in yard) can be destroyed by pouring a kettle or pan of boiling water down each opening.

A fairly effective ant stopper is ordinary white vinegar. Wash down any areas where you see ants with full strength vinegar and let the area air dry. Don't forget to wipe down around the windows in the kitchen.

To keep ants from coming inside, mix two

cups of borax with one cup of sugar and sprinkle it around the foundation of the house.

The best defense against ants is to not feed them. Keep any crumbs or other small pieces of food wiped up. Ants come into the house looking for food and water.

Another way to keep ants out of the house is to place whole cloves where they enter. Also tuck a few in the back of your kitchen cabinets and under the kitchen sink.

Ants are also deterred by dried coffee grounds. Sprinkle used coffee grounds outside near the doorways and around any windows, to help keep the ants away.

Smart Reader Solution:
I was puzzled years ago to see my mother-in-law carrying orange and grapefruit rinds into the yard and carefully placing them cut side down near plants in her garden. She explained to me that the rinds become traps for slugs and snails. The citrus rinds attract the little beasties who cling to the interior. This makes it possible to gather them up, place them in a plastic bag, and put the whole package in the garbage. No damage to the environment; no danger to pets from poisonous bait; very little mess; and the price is right. I have taken this further by eliminating the plastic bag. I just dump the sails and

pests out in a place where I can squash them and reuse the traps until they warrant a place in the compost heap.

Q. How can I get rid of moths? I've tried cedar and moth balls (what a smell). The moths disappear for a short time and are back again. They are in my closet and my kitchen. I even put all of my perishables in the refrigerator. Please help.

A. Dried bay leaves offer a good, inexpensive moth protection. Scatter dried bay leaves in the drawers and between layers of clothing in your closet. This is especially important when you pack them away for storage. In your kitchen place a leaf or two on each shelf where moths are a problem.

Q. How can I keep meal worms out of my food? It is very expensive to throw the food away when the worms get to it before I do.

A. Meal worms, which are attracted to open packages of macaroni, noodles or spaghetti, are repelled by spearmint chewing gum. You won't be bothered by these pests if you place a few sticks of wrapped gum in or near the packages. Be sure to leave the gum wrapped so that it won't dry out and lose the spearmint scent.

To keep the gnats away while you're outside, rub a thin layer of baby oil on all exposed skin. For mosquitoes, rub a little cider vinegar on exposed skin.

To kill flying insects, use inexpensive hair spray. The hair spray will harden their wings so they cannot fly. They will drop like flies!

Keep ants away from the food on your picnic table by placing each table leg into a bucket or plastic bowl filled with water. The ants cannot swim, so they will leave your picnic food alone!

12

Best Buys Calendar

SKINFLINT BEST BUYS CALENDAR

Smart shoppers know when to shop for the lowest prices. Lower your grocery bill by taking advantage of in season produce. Keep your total spending down by shopping when you can find the best sales. Many stores will stick to these traditional sale dates. Happy bargain hunting!

January

Beef, Broccoli, Brussels Sprouts, Chicken, Eggs, Grapefruit, Oranges, Pork, Rhubarb, Turnips, Christmas Decorations, White Sales (Linens, Towels, etc.), Bedding, Holiday Clothes, Women's Clothes, Gifts, Stationery, Radios, Appliances, China, Home Furnishings, Art Supplies, Bicycles, Costume Jewelry, Electronic Equipment, Lingerie

February

Apples, Broccoli, Chicken, Fish, Oranges, Oysters, Rhubarb, Scallops, Strawberries, Turnips, Housewares, Men's Clothing, Shoes, Toys, Coats, Large Appliances, Bedding, Furniture, Curtains, Sportswear, Lamps, Rugs, Carpet

March

Apples, Artichokes, Beef, Broccoli, Chicken, Eggs, Fish, Grapefruit, Lamb, Oranges, Pineapple, Rhubarb, Scallops, Turnips, Coats, Appliances, China, Glassware, Ski Equipment, Typewriters, Storm Windows, Hosiery, Luggage, Children's Shoes, Children's Clothing

April

Artichokes, Asparagus, Broccoli, Chicken, Eggs, Fish, Grapefruit, Lamb, Lemons, Pineapple, Pork, Rhubarb, Summer Squash, Turkey, Dresses, Hats, Men's Suits, Patio Furniture, Air Conditioners, Shoes, Vacuum Cleaners, Easter Candy, Infants' Wear

May

Asparagus, Beans, Beef, Broccoli, Corn, Cucumbers, Eggs, Fish, Lamb, Lemons, Peas, Pineapple, Pork, Rhubarb, Strawberries, Summer Squash, Tomatoes, Tires, Snow Tires, Lingerie, Summer Clothes, Handbags, Housewares, Boys' Clothing, Men's Clothing, Blankets, Bathrobes, TV Sets, Handbags

June

Apricots, Asparagus, Beans, Beef, Beets, Berries, Cherries, Corn, Cucumbers, Eggs, Fish, Lemons, Melons, Peas, Plums, Radishes, Salmon, Summer Squash, Tomatoes, Women's Sportswear, Furniture, Luggage, Lingerie, Summer Sportswear, Building Materials

July
Apricots, Beans, Beets, Berries, Cherries, Corn, Cucumbers, Grapes, Fish, Lemons, Limes, Melons, Nectarines, Plums, Peppers, Squash, Tomatoes, Watermelon, Underwear, Shoes, Men's Summer Suits, Bathing Suits, Air Conditioners, Fuel Oil, Home Appliances

August
Beans, Chicken, Corn, Eggplant, Fish, Grapes, Melons, Lemons, Peaches, Pears, Plums, Peppers, Summer Squash, Tomatoes, Watermelon, Furniture, Carpet, Linens, Air Conditioners, Gardening Tools, Patio Furniture. New Cars, Camping Equipment, Home Furnishings

September
Beef, Beets, Broccoli, Cauliflower, Chicken , Clams, Corn, Eggplant, Fish, Grapes, Peaches, Pears, Peppers, Plums, Scallops, Tomatoes, Housewares, Hardware, Garden Supplies, Children's Clothes, Automobiles, Bathing Suits, Car batteries, Dishes, Mufflers, Paint

October
Apples, Beans, Beef, Beets, Broccoli, Brussels Sprouts, Cauliflower, Chestnuts, Cranberries, Parsnips, Pears, Pork, Pumpkin, Scallops, Sweet Potatoes, Turkey, Turnips, Winter Squash, Women's Winter Clothes, Hosiery, Lingerie, Major appliances, Silverware, Camping Equipment, Glassware, School Supplies

November

Apples, Beef, Broccoli, Brussels Sprouts,
Cauliflower, Chestnuts, Cranberries, Fish,
Lamb, Oranges, Oysters, Pears, Pumpkin,
Sweet Potatoes, Tangelos, Tangerines, Turkey,
Turnips, Winter Squash, Blankets, Dresses,
Water Heaters, Men's Shoes, Women's Fall
Clothes

December

Apples, Broccoli, Brussels Sprouts, Chicken,
Cranberries, Grapefruit, Lamb, Oranges,
Oysters, Pork, Sweet Potatoes, Tangelos,
Tangerines, Turkey, Turnips, Winter Squash,
Used Cars, Christmas & Party Items, Hats,
Infants' Needs, Boy's Suits, Men's Clothing

Carrots, Celery, Onions and Potatoes are
good buys throughout the entire year.

13

Quick & Thrifty Formulas

Try these quick and thrifty formulas to save money all around the house!

Jewelry Cleaner

For an inexpensive jewelry cleaner mix equal parts ammonia and warm water. Soak jewelry for 5 to 10 minutes. Use an old toothbrush to clean any hard to reach spots. Let dry without rinsing.

Facial Cleanser

Mix half a cup of mayonnaise with one tablespoon melted butter and the juice of one lemon. Place the face cream in a glass jar and store in the refrigerator. Just take a little out and use it to clean your face and remove any makeup. This will clean and soften your skin. Rinse your face with cold water after cleaning with this homemade formula. One batch will last for a long time.

Cream Deodorant

To make cream deodorant, mix 2 teaspoons of baking soda, 2 teaspoons of petroleum jelly and 2 teaspoons of talcum powder. Heat in a double boiler over low heat and stir until a smooth cream forms. Cool and transfer to a small container with a tight lid.

Starch

Make your own inexpensive spray starch for ironing clothes by adding one tablespoon cornstarch to two cups of water. If you prefer a heavier starch, add two or three tablespoons of starch. Pour the mixture into a spray bottle. Shake the mixture before each use.

Laundry Booster

Add 1/2 cup white vinegar
or 1/2 cup baking soda

Homemade Stain Remover

You may never have to buy pre-treating stain remover again! It really works.

1/2 cup ammonia
/2 cup white vinegar
1/4 cup baking soda
2 tablespoons liquid soap
2 quarts water

Mix all ingredients together and pour into a spray bottle. Spray the solution on the stain and let it soak for a few minutes before washing as usual. Shake the solution before each use.

Window Cleaner
Mix:
1 pint water
1/2 cup alcohol
1 tablespoon ammonia
blue food coloring (optional)

Pour into an empty spray bottle.

All purpose Cleaner
1 tablespoon liquid dishwashing soap
Clear ammonia

Pour the dishwashing soap into a spray bottle
and add enough ammonia to fill the bottle.
Use it for cleaning counters, appliances, windows and just about anything else around the
house!

Toilet Cleaner
1 part baking soda to one part mild detergent

Disinfectant
1/2 cup borax in 1 gallon of water

Drain Cleaner
First pour boiling water
follow with 1/4 cup baking soda
next pour 2 ounces of vinegar

Floor & Furniture Polish
1 part lemon juice
1 part olive/vegetable oil

138

Ant Traps

These are safe, nonpoisonous traps.

1/4 cup sugar
1/4 cup baking yeast
1/2 cup molasses
small index cards (3X5 inch)

Mix sugar, yeast and molasses in a small bowl. Smear a thin layer of the mixture on each index card with a spatula. Place the cards, syrup side up, in areas where ants travel.

Baby Wipes

1 roll of paper towels
   (cut in half so you have 2 small rolls)
1 to 1 1/2 cup water
1 tablespoon baby shampoo
1 tablespoon oil (baby or canola)

Take one of the smaller rolls and soak with liquid mixture. Use an empty plastic baby wipes container. When towels are soaked through, remove the cardboard tube and pull wipes from the center. You may need to add more liquid. Save the other small roll of paper towels for next time.

Rainbow Chunk Crayons

Recycle old crayon stubs by melting them and making creative new crayons.

Supplies needed: Old crayon pieces; empty clean soup or vegetable cans (Pinch one side to form a pouring spout); saucepan; water; paper muffin liners and a muffin tin.

Adult supervision required for this project.

Peel wrappers from crayons. Sort crayons by colors (if desired). Fill an empty, clean soup can about half full of broken crayon pieces. Fill the saucepan with about 2 inches of water. Heat the water over medium heat. Place the can of crayons in the water and allow them to melt. When crayons are melted to a liquid wax, pour about 1/2 inch wax into each muffin liner. If you melt several colors you can swirl the colors to make a pretty design.

Cool the new crayons by placing them into the refrigerator or freezer. You can add several different colored layers to the new crayons. Peel away the paper liners when crayons are completely cool and hard.

Lawn Fertilizer

1 cup Epsom salts
1 cup household ammonia

Combine in a clean jar. To use, mix two table-spoons of the mixture with 2 gallons of water in a watering can and sprinkle over 150 to 200 square feet of turf. Or if you prefer to use a hose sprayer, mix the entire batch with enough water to make one quart of liquid. Pour the liquid into the sprayer. A quart of diluted fertilizer will cover about 2,500 square feet.

Driveway Cleaner

This formula works for oil, grease, or trans-mission fluid that drips from your car onto a concrete surface. Here's what you'll need:

Paint thinner   Cat litter   Broom

Pour paint thinner straight from the can on the spots. Saturate the spots as well as an area 6 to 12 inches beyond them. Then, spread a thick layer of cat litter over the entire area treated so that you cannot see the con-crete surface. Let the cat litter stand for about an hour to absorb the greasy stains. Then use a broom to sweep up the soiled cat litter. Some older stains may require two applica-tions. Be sure to ventilate the area if you are working inside the garage or patio.

Ice Packs

Ice packs are easy and inexpensive to make. Simply mix one part rubbing alcohol with two parts water. The alcohol and water mixture will not freeze solid; it stays slushy and can be shaped around difficult places such as knees or elbows. To make a small ice pack use a quart-sized plastic storage bag that seals shut ("Zip Lock" type bag). Pour one cup rubbing alcohol and two cups water into the bag and seal it shut. Squeeze out as much air as possible before you press the bag closed. Place the bag in the freezer and leave it there until you need it. You can re-use these bags many times; after using, simply place the bag back into the freezer for next time. To make a large ice pack, use a gallon-size bag and double the recipe.

Skinflint Newspaper Clipping

To preserve a newspaper clipping, dissolve a milk of magnesia tablet in a quart of club soda and let it sit overnight. The next day pour the mixture into a pan large enough to hold the flattened newspaper clipping. Soak the clipping for one hour; remove and gently pat dry. Place the clipping on a flat surface and do not move until completely dry. The estimated life of your clipping after the milk of magnesia treatment is 200 years!

14

Skinflint Recipes

Easy Sweet Condensed Milk

In saucepan:
1/3 cup plus 2 tablespoons evaporated milk
1 cup sugar
3 tablespoons butter

Heat until blended and use as you would a can of sweetened condensed milk. This is similar to Eagle Brand and other brands of canned sweetened condensed milk.

Pancake Syrup

3 cups brown sugar
1 1/2 cups water
1 teaspoon vanilla

Combine ingredients in a saucepan. Bring mixture to a boil and stir until sugar dissolves. Store leftover syrup in the refrigerator. Heat the leftover syrup in the microwave or on the stove top before serving again.

Sour Cream Substitute

Mix 3/4 cup plain yogurt
1/3 cup instant dry milk
1 teaspoon cornstarch (for baking)

Use this recipe to replace one cup sour cream.

144

Mom's Tender Turkey Recipe

1 small turkey (8 to 12 pounds)
1 stick of margarine
1 quartered onion
3 sliced celery stalks
water
poultry seasoning
salt and pepper

Place the turkey (completely thawed) in a
roaster with a tight fitting lid. Melt the
margarine and brush over the turkey. Place
the celery and onions inside the turkey cavity.
Season with poultry seasoning and salt and
pepper. Pour 1 to 2 inches of water in the
roaster. Preheat oven to 500 degrees. When
the oven is preheated, place the turkey in the
oven for 1 hour for 8 to 10 pounds or 1 hour
and 15 minutes for 10 to 12 pounds. After the
hour (or hour and 15 minutes), turn the oven
off but leave the turkey in the oven for
another hour. Leave the lid on during the
second hour. Before carving, take the lid off
for 15 to 20 minutes.

Vinegar Pie

1/2 cup margarine melted and cooled
3 eggs slightly beaten
1/4 cup vinegar
1 1/4 cup sugar
2 tablespoons flour
1 tablespoon vanilla
1 9 inch pie shell (homemade or frozen)

Preheat the oven to 325 degrees. Mix the margarine, eggs, vinegar, sugar, flour, and vanilla in a bowl until well blended. Bake the pie for about one hour at 325 degrees. Check it a few minutes before the hour. The filling should be light brown when it is done. Allow the pie to cool before cutting it into slices. It is delicious cold or warmed up in the microwave.

Easy Barbecue Sauce

Mix together:
1 LB brown sugar
1 #10 can catsup
2 oz. coarsely ground pepper
1 5 oz. bottle Worcestershire
1 4 oz. bottle liquid smoke

Refrigerate and enjoy!

Skinflint Wacky Cake

1 teaspoon baking soda
1 cup sugar
2 tablespoons cocoa
1 1/2 cups flour
1/4 teaspoon salt
1 tablespoon vinegar
1 tablespoon vanilla
1 tablespoon cooking oil
1 cup water

Mix baking soda, sugar, cocoa, flour and salt together; sift into an 8"X8" cake pan. Make 3 holes in the mixture and pour the vinegar, vanilla and cooking oil into the holes, separately. Pour the water over the whole mixture, then mix until lumps are out. Bake at 350 degrees for 30 to 35 minutes or until toothpick comes out clean.

Better Butter

1 pound softened butter
2 cups skim milk
1 envelope unflavored gelatin

Mix gelatin and 1 cup skim milk in a pan. Place over low heat until gelatin is dissolved. Blend in butter. Add the second cup of skim milk and mix thoroughly. Refrigerate.
Note: If you do not like the texture of this recipe add more butter. It will spread better if allowed to soften slightly before using.

Homemade Egg Substitute

6 egg whites
1 tablespoon oil
1/4 cup powdered milk

Combine all ingredients in a mixing bowl and blend smooth or use a blender. Store in a jar in the refrigerator. It will store up to one week in the refrigerator. It also freezes well. You can add a drop of yellow coloring to make it look more like "real" eggs. You can use this in recipes calling for eggs. One fourth (1/4) cup equals one whole egg.
To prepare scrambled eggs, fry mixture slowly over low heat in a non-stick fry pan.
This is similar to Egg Beaters brand and other low cholesterol egg substitutes.

Skinflint No-Pecan Pecan Pie

1 Stick butter, melted
3/4 cup sugar
2 eggs
3/4 cup dark corn syrup
1 tsp. vanilla
1 cup uncooked oats
unbaked 9" pie crust

Preheat oven to 350 degrees. Mix together butter, sugar, eggs, syrup and vanilla. Add oats and blend. Pour into crust and bake for 50 to 55 minutes or until knife inserted near center comes out clean.

Shake It And Bake It Coating

2 cups sifted all-purpose flour
1 tablespoon seasoned salt
4 teaspoons onion powder
1 tablespoon paprika
1 teaspoon salt
1 teaspoon black pepper

Put all ingredients in a paper or plastic bag.
Close the bag and shake to mix the ingredients. Store in an airtight container. The coating will last about 6 months. This recipe is
enough to coat 20-25 pork chops or 4 to 5
chickens. Pour just the amount of coating you
will need for one meal in a bag. You can always add more if you do not have enough. Do
not pour any leftover coating back into the jar
with the fresh coating after you have dipped
the raw meat into it.

Fried Green Tomatoes

Growing up in a suburb of Atlanta, Georgia
during the summer fried green tomatoes
would appear on our dinner table quite frequently. To make fried green tomatoes: Slice
the green tomatoes and dip them in milk.
Then dip them in flour seasoned with salt and
pepper. Let the tomatoes sit for 5 minutes and
dip them again in the flour mixture. Fry over
medium heat until brown, about 2 minutes on
each side. Serve hot from the grill. Not only
are they different and delicious but a great
way to use up all those extra tomatoes!

Pudding Mix

3 1/3 cups dry milk
2 1/3 teaspoon salt
1 tablespoon corn starch
1 2/3 cups sugar

Combine dry ingredients and store in a tightly closed container. This recipe is enough for 4 batches of pudding.

Vanilla Pudding:
Combine 1 1/4 cups of dry mix with 1/34 cups water. Cook over low heat to a boil, stirring constantly. Boil gently for 2 minutes. Add one teaspoon vanilla. Chill until set.

Chocolate Pudding:
Add 4 tablespoons cocoa to dry ingredients before mixing.

The Skinflint News
Monthly Newsletter

SKIN-FLINT: A thrifty-minded person who saves money by all means possible. He also recycles to save money and the environment.

If you liked *Smart Solutions*, you'll love the *Skinflint News* monthly newsletter. It's packed full of money-saving tips and strategies to help you make ends meet all year long!

To subscribe to the *Skinflint News*, fill out the coupon below and send a $12.00 check or money order. You'll get 12 issues (one full year) for just a buck an issue!

The Skinflint News
P. O. Box 818
Palm Harbor, FL 34682-0818

✓ Yes, I want to be a Skinflint, too! My check or money order for $12.00 is enclosed.

Name:_____
Address:_____
City:_____
State, Zip:_____

The Grocery Guide

Cut your Grocery Bill In Half!
Tons of Tremendous Tips!
Lots of Smart Strategies!
Bundles of Fabulous Freebies!

Over 100 tips and strategies to help slash hundreds or even thousands of dollars off your annual grocery bill. Get $10 in **FREE** grocery coupons! Free recipes, seeds, produce, cleaning supplies and much more!

152